A Foot
Remen

SOUTHERN

Jacket illustrations

Front: Converted 'West Country' class Pacific, No. 34048 *Crediton,* on the 'up' main line between Farnborough and Woking, at Pirbright Junction. The flyover line to Alton via Aldershot is carried by the bridge above the train.

Rear: Driver Tom Flight prepares to start the 12.05p.m. Reading to Redhill service on the last day of steam working to Redhill, 1st January 1965. Tom was one of Reading's characters.

A Footplateman Remembers the

SOUTHERN

J. A. Rowe

Oxford Publishing Co.

Typesetting by:
Aquarius Typesetting Services, New Milton, Hants.

Printed in Great Britain by:
Hollen Street Press Ltd, Slough, Berks.

Published by:
Oxford Publishing Co.
Link House
West Street
POOLE, Dorset

Contents

Acknowledgements

I dedicate this book to Cathryn, who carried out all my typing, and whose general assistance was of such great help to me. Thanks also to my son, Adrian, who carried and fetched material between myself and Cathryn. Grateful thanks are also due to Cyril Wilson, my brother Jack, my son Jim, Brian Chiswell, Peter and Gary, the Berkshire County Library, and last, but certainly not least, to my wife for putting up with my writing exploits through the long winter evenings, when I forgot to make the tea.

CHAPTER ONE

We All Have to Learn

Having completed 45½ years in the footplate line of promotion on the Southern Region of British Railways, it occurs to me that I should have something of interest to put into words. I know of many men who have worked for as many years in various types of employment, and often some interesting and valuable historical information has been lost forever because their experiences were never set down.

In moving from engine cleaner at sixteen years of age, to being passed to act as driver in 1949, my period as a fireman included the years of World War II, and the varied types of motive power that I have been involved with over the years have disappeared or are due to be scrapped. Because of the nature of the job, my story is bound to have a parochial appearance in terms of railway mileage and boundaries, but it was always my opinion that whatever region or types of traction one worked on, the responsibilities and difficulties were in many ways similar.

It may help the prospective reader if my family background and upbringing is explained, because there is no doubt in my mind that the schooling, the type of teachers we had and even the type of work we did all tended to affect our character and general outlook on life. I was born in August 1920 at Crowthorne, on the south-east borders of Berkshire, I am the eldest but one of ten children, — five boys and five girls — and I started attending Crowthorne Church School in 1925. Possibly one of the most respected men that Crowthorne ever knew was the schoolmaster Mr Goodband, who was a native of Derbyshire and also came to the school in 1925. It is not until many years afterwards that one realises how much is owed to men like Mr Goodband; he fostered in me an appreciation of the area in which I lived, simply by talking about the Derbyshire Dales where his own roots obviously were. My father, a native of Wokingham, was a railway porter who had been wounded in France in 1917, later being invalided to Birmingham in 1918 where he met and married my mother.

I cannot claim to be the typical boy who wanted to be an engine driver, in fact, I still have a vivid memory, as a boy of five, of standing in awe and dread on Birmingham (Snow Hill) Station looking up at a monster called *Evesham Abbey*. I wondered then how those two men had the courage to stand on that footplate. My only other experience of steam engines was as a nine year old in 1929, when the 'Schools' class engine No. 902 *Wellington* (named after the local college) was on view at Crowthorne Station; again it seemed a tremendous machine for two men to take charge of. We learnt that the driver was Bill Deacon and the fireman was Albert Simms. I had no idea then that I would eventually work on the footplate with both of these men.

During my school-days, my interest was in aircraft. The Cody Air Circus was often flying in the area and the Flying Flea, which was little more than a two-stroke motor bike with wings and a tail, regularly flew around Crowthorne. My heroes then were Stainforth and Waghorn, and the men who flew the Supermarine Seaplane to win the Schneider Trophy for England.

Leaving school in August 1934, I was pleased to obtain a job at the Phillips & Powis Aircraft Factory in Woodley, near Reading, and although it meant cycling ten miles morning and evening for 9s. 6d. a week, I was happy working on aircraft. I started making aileron ribs in a jig and after a few months was upgraded and went on to making wing ribs. After about a year I was put as assistant on main tail plane assembly with a kindly man named Mr Owen; he was instrumental in helping me to mould my own opinions of life in general, but he was an expert carpenter and I felt that I could never aspire to his skills.

The Miles Hawk aircraft we produced were monoplanes with a Cirrus engine, and they were treated with a coat of blood red stuff called 'dope'; men working in the 'dope shop' had to drink two pints of milk a day. After being treated the plane would be wheeled out on to the tarmac and the test pilot, Tommy Rose, would taxi to a position, take off and fly the plane. We understood that the engine and all controls were tested, ending with a terminal velocity dive over the aerodrome, after which the plane could be given a license number and painted.

Some time in November 1935, or around that time, I was approached by Management to take on main tail plane assembly for almost a doubling of my wages. I agreed that I could do the job, and was elated to think that I was going to be trusted with the responsibility. On the pay day of that week I walked through the hangar and saw Mr Owen on the other side of a fuselage — he looked right 'down in the mouth' as though he had been crying. I asked a man named Stevenson if he knew what was wrong with Mr Owen. 'What's wrong with him' he said, 'He's got the sack, and you've taken his b . . . . y job'. I cycled home that evening with a heavy heart, and never went back to Reading Aerodrome again. I could only hope that Mr Owen would retain his job.

During 1935, my elder brother Jack had started as an engine cleaner at Guildford Locomotive Shed, and through talking to him I started to get an interest in railways, and managed to get recorded at Guildford Shed as a prospective employee. In the meantime I had several jobs around the village during 1936 — butcher's assistant and milk roundsman being examples, — and was working as an under gardener when the railway notified me to attend for a medical examination for footplate duties. After passing the medical examination, I was then required to supply three character references. These were duly obtained, and I was notified to start cleaning at Guildford Shed on 20th April 1937.

Guildford Shed was a round shed, and access to all roads under cover was only obtained by going on to the turntable, which was then moved to the particular road in which the engine was required. The office buildings were joined to what was referred to as the old shed; this was the area for 'dead' engines, i.e. engines out of steam for boilersmiths, boilerwashers and engine fitters to carry out periodical examinations, and to attend to steam blows or regulator glands reported by drivers. Adjustment of brakes and the changing of brake-blocks was also attended to in the old shed, and it was here that engine cleaners often worked — especially during the day shift. If enough interest was shown, the fitters and boilersmiths would explain things and answer questions, so that a good knowledge of the make-up of a steam locomotive could be obtained. Some of the men I talked to then had been working on steam engines in the 1890s, and they had needed to adjust to many changes of locomotive design as engines became bigger and faster. The mess-rooms for shed staff (cleaners, firemen and drivers) were also in the old shed, while the new shed completed the rest of the circle. I have no idea when it was added, but this was the area for live engines that were ready for duty as required; fitters were sometimes required to attend to minor faults in this area.

The coaling plant and the area for disposal of engines was to the north of the engine sheds, almost alongside platform 8 at Guildford Station. Engines progressed from this area to the turntable, where the shed turner was responsible for placing them for available access, as he had the knowledge of when they were next required.

The whole area, from the coaling plant to the engine sheds, is now a car-park. Guildford Shed had obviously been hewn out of a hill of chalk, known as St. Catherine's Hill; this hill was of sufficient altitude to justify the building of a tunnel, which commences within about 100 yards south of the station and is about three quarters of a mile in length. This line is the continuation of the line from Waterloo to Portsmouth, with a junction about two miles from Guildford, at Shalford, which is the continuation of the old South Eastern main line from Reading to London Bridge, via Redhill.

There were between seventy and eighty cleaners at Guildford during 1937 and at that time I was the youngest, but there were married men around forty years of age who were often used as firemen, but who were still only designated cleaners. Most of them proudly wore the brass cap badge in their hats, and kept them polished. This badge denoted that they had completed 313 firing duties, and when they were back as cleaners they were paid the lowest fireman's rate of pay which was 9s. 6d. a day. As a cleaner it was 4s. 0d. a day which increased at 1s. 0d. a day at seventeen years of age, on up to 8s. 0d. a day at twenty years of age. A total of 313 firing duties was the agreed number, this being based on one year's work as a fireman less 52 Sundays but, of course, at that time, some men had taken up to ten years before they were paid the lowest fireman's rate, when put back as cleaners.

Generally a gang of eight to twelve cleaners worked on an engine, each being responsible for his particular part. This meant two on the boiler and smokebox, two on cab and framing paintwork, two on the tender, two on the wheels (and the area behind the wheels called the back framings) and two on the motions (side rods, big ends, little ends and all exposed parts which were mechanical). If the engine was of the type with an inside motion, then the cleaner would work underneath. It was instilled into us that a good cleaner became a good driver. To see an engine properly cleaned and ready for service at that time gave us a feeling of pride, and we felt the job was worthwhile.

I well remember being part of a gang during 1937, when King George VI was going to Portsmouth on the Royal Train, for the review of the fleet at Spithead. The Royal Train engine was No. 119 — a Class T9 engine based at Nine Elms Shed but in the event that this engine broke down or had any trouble at all, Guildford was responsible for supplying a standby engine of the same class. We were instructed to work on engine No. 709, which was to be the Royal standby engine, and when we had finished the engine was moved on to the turntable for the passing of the Royal Train. She looked beautiful, with the long copper injector pipes, from the clack box on the side of the boiler, down to the injector below the cab. When these copper pipes were really burnished with brick dust and the copper safety-valves on the dome were also treated the same, with all paintwork spotlessly shining, a Class T9 engine looked better than any other I have seen.

I believe it had been the practice at most depots where many cleaners were employed for new recruits to undergo some sort of initiation ceremony. At Guildford it was the 'Chalk Hole Goblins' that the junior cleaner was introduced to, and the visit into the tunnel to meet the 'Goblins' was always done when on night work. Fortunately for me this practise had been discontinued in 1937; this was because men were often working in the tunnel, as the track was being made ready for the electric service to Portsmouth that would eventually replace the steam service in September of that year. The mythical 'Goblins' were never visited by me, although I heard plenty of talk about them. I think the idea was for several experienced cleaners to go into the tunnel where they would hide up in the safety alcoves, while others took the new boy into the tunnel and did their best to leave him stranded. He then had to run the gauntlet of the 'Goblins' in the alcoves to get back to the locomotive shed.

One other job that Guildford cleaners did was night work at Bordon, which was the terminus of a small branch line from Bentley, between Farnham and Alton. At Bordon the Longmoor Military Railway commenced, and ran through some pretty Hampshire countryside almost to Liss, on the main Portsmouth line. The job at Bordon meant cleaning the engine, which was kept busy all day working push-pull trains over the branch lines. It was always a Class M7 tank engine, specially fitted for push-pull work so that the driver could drive from the leading coach. This meant that when travelling bunker first, the fireman was on the footplate on his own. The cleaner at Bordon also got 6d. extra each night for coaling the engine for the next day's duty, and it was always the practice to oil the axle and all other parts for the early turn driver.

The very busy time for Guildford Shed was in June, and throughout three weeks in June 1937 I was booked out as a fireman. The Aldershot Tattoo and Ascot Races created a lot of work, with special traffic being very heavy, and at the same time, about twelve drivers were being trained to drive electric trains which meant that their steam duties had to be covered. During this three week period when performing fireman's duties, my pay moved from 4s. 0d. a day to 9s. 6d. a day. Most of my duties then were with the driver responsible for moving engines from the coal stage to the engine sheds.

11

In September 1937, with the inception of the electric service on the Waterloo to Portsmouth line, the loss of work caused me and about ten other cleaners to be made redundant, although I was fortunate, as I was to be transferred to Reading which was nearer to my home, at Crowthorne, than Guildford. What concerned me most was that I would no longer see those lovely 'Schools' class engines, which had run regularly through Guildford on the London to Portsmouth service. I knew them all — *Blundell's, Malvern, Radley, Merchant Taylors, King's-Wimbledon, King's-Canterbury, Christ's Hospital, Haileybury* and many others. These engines were considered to be the most powerful four-coupled engines in Europe, and I can well believe that this was true, as I eventually got round to driving some of them.

I was leaving a depot that had been part of the London & South Western Railway, and was moving to a depot that had been part of the London & South Eastern Railway. Although the railways had grouped to form the Southern Railway in 1923, along with the London, Brighton & South Coast Railway and the London, Chatham & Dover Railway, I was surprised by the fierce and sometimes foolish loyalty to the men and engines of the railway they had originally worked for. With the many types of locomotive that became the property of the Southern Railway, it was inevitable that men had to work on strange engines, and some found it very difficult to adjust.

An important person in any locomotive depot at that time was the steam raiser, whose duties included looking after the fires of engines in steam and making sure that the water level of the boilers was maintained. If he was good at his job he could be an asset to drivers and firemen signing on at all times of the day and night. Before preparing an engine for service, it was a great help if the water level in the gauge glass was showing just above half-way, with a good fire in the back of the firebox which could be pushed all over the grate area of the firebox. About 100lb. pressure of steam was enough to move the engine for oiling purposes, and this allowed the fireman to maintain control of the boiler, while at the same time building up the fire to enable the engine to be set back on to any train with a good head of steam, and a fire that would allow the driver to work the engine in any position according to gradient and load. Another important duty of steam raisers was to light-up engines which had been stopped for boiler washing and for attention to leaking stays or seams in the firebox. The engine was always cold, and it would take about three to four hours to get the engine in steam.

On settling down at Reading at the end of 1937, I was surprised by the different method of lighting-up engines from the way I had seen it done at Guildford, and although it was fourteen years since the Grouping of the railways, Guildford had retained the L&SWR system, while Reading had retained the SECR system. At Guildford the steam raiser used firelighters, these being five or six sticks of wood formed into an oblong-shaped box, and packed tight with paraffin-soaked wood shavings. They were about 6in. long, and 3in. wide and deep. The steam raiser would line the front and sides of the firebox with coal, causing the air to come up through the firebars in the middle of the firebox, several firelighters, being slow burning, were dropped in the middle of the firebox. When they were well alight, fist-sized lumps of coal were shovelled on to the burning firelighters and within about an hour, the coal at the front and sides of the box would ignite through convected heat. At Reading a large furnace was kept burning at all times, and a large scoop-like shovel was used by the steam raiser to carry burning red hot coal to the footplate of the engine. After two or three trips, enough fire would have been put into the firebox, and coal would be added to this until a good fire was obtained. The furnace would then be made up ready to be used for the next engine that required lighting-up. This furnace was about 2ft. from ground level, and was always kept well-charged with coal by the cleaners. We all used to practise swinging a shovelful of coal into the fire, practising for the time when we would be doing it on the footplate, but there was considerable difference between a stationary firebox and the firebox of a working locomotive.

The furnace, in fact, served a dual purpose. Above it was a fine mesh sieve on which damp sand was shovelled, and as the sand dried out it fell into a large aluminium box with sloping sides, which narrowed as it fell lower. At about a foot from ground level a sliding flap was fitted, this being at the level of a correctly-designed sand bucket, so that when the bucket was placed below the flap and the flap lifted, the hot sand ran into the bucket almost at the rate of running water. The testing of sanding gear and equipment was an important part of the fireman's preparation duties, and it was his job also to fill all sand-boxes. This was a heavy job because after carrying the sand from the furnace, it had then to be lifted to the top framings of the engine where the sand-boxes were generally situated. This was the obvious and simple method of using gravity to sand the rail when the sanding equipment was operated from the footplate. One lesson we learnt early as fireman, was never to operate the sanding gear whilst the engine was slipping, but always to wait until the driver closed the regulator, shutting off power to the pistons so that the driving wheels were moving along the rail and not spinning on it.

During winter months it was quite common for 'dossers' or tramps to find their way up to the locomotive deopt at Reading, and have a warm night's rest at the back of the sand furnace. They were usually left undisturbed, but there was one steam raiser who couldn't resist the challenge of creeping quietly up to the sleeping tramp and tying his bootlaces together. It wasn't done with any malice, but he knew it always amused the cleaners to be safe on the footplate of a nearby engine when the 'dosser' was woken up by someone banging the other side of the furnace with a shovel. These tramps or 'dossers' never left the locomotive shed without a hot cup of tea from someone on duty or a sandwich of some sort. I am sure they used to pass the word to each other that they could get a night's rest and a breakfast at Reading (Southern) Locomotive Shed.

There were only three roads under cover at Reading Shed, and the back end of the middle road was always used for washing out engines and for attention to firebox seams and stays. When all plugs had been safely replaced a hydrant hose was fixed to the injector waste water pipe, and when the water was turned on it was forced up the injector pipe, through the clack valve on the side of the boiler and into the boiler. The engine was then shunted out to the back pit outside the shed, close to the sand furnace, and was now ready for lighting-up.

Sometime around 1952, Stirling Class F1 No. 1140 was lit-up by the late turn steam raiser at about 7p.m. There was really no need for him to go on to the engine again, as his day was finished at 10p.m., and he had obviously made a good fire up so that the engine would start to make steam soon after he went off duty. The night steam raiser signed on duty at 10p.m., and with engines in steam to attend to it was about 11.15p.m. when he got around to looking at No. 1140. When he held the cabside handrail he soon let go of it as it was almost red hot, and when he looked from the ground the exterior plugs over the crown of the firebox were glowing red hot. It was obvious to him that No. 1140 had been lit-up with no water in the boiler. Arrangements were quickly made for a fireman to throw the fire out and, with the use of thick leather gloves, it was not too long a job despite his working in surroundings of a high temperature, with the sides of the cab being hot and parts of the boiler front on the footplate starting to glow. We all thought this must be the end of No. 1140 which was a shame, as I had a bit of a soft spot for her as she had been the regular engine of Driver Bill Chown, who I had fired to from 1944 to 1947. When the service from Reading to Waterloo was worked by steam before January 1939, I had covered his regular mate's holiday for one week on No. 1140 and, at that time, it had been a very important job for one so inexperienced; this would have been around 1938. The top boilersmith on the region had to visit Reading to examine No. 1140 and, with a complete change of all boiler plugs and a renewal of stays and seams in the firebox, to everyone's surprise No. 1140 was passed fit for service. What was even more amazing was that afterwards No. 1140 became a much freer steaming engine; although the Class F1s were free steamers this one was never any trouble no matter what the load. She was also a much stronger engine than any other of the class. The F1s were pressed at 160lb., – that is they would start to blow at the safety-valves when the pressure gauge reached 160lb., but No. 1140 would go to 173lb. before she started to whimper at the safety-valves and it was 175lb. before she started to ramp.

I was driving regularly at this time of course, and worked over the Redhill road many times with her. It was the extra steam pressure that made her a better engine, but I must admit that if she started ramping at the safety-valves and my mind wandered back to what she had been through, I sometimes felt a bit uneasy and was always glad when the safety-valves went quiet. The generally-accepted explanation for the change was that No. 1140 had been at Reading since the early 1920s and Reading water is notoriously hard; anyone boiling a kettle regularly in Reading can substantiate this, as the kettle will soon obtain a thick wall of limestone fur. If this is multiplied over many years and the millions of gallons of water that No. 1140 had boiled, it can be assumed that there was a fair coating of limestone inside the boiler, and that the application of direct heat, without water, had caused this to break up and free itself from the inside of the boiler, thus improving her steaming qualities.

Just one more incident is worthy of mention before leaving the sand furnaces. The coal supplied at Reading for the furnace was of the very lowest quality, being full of dirt, and the only engines that could be coaled with it were the yard shunting tanks Nos. 1047 and 1070. They would go out at 6a.m., and if they kept going the firebox would be solid with clinker by 10p.m. This low grade coal came from Tilmanstone Colliery in Kent, and it was said that it was being mined about 300 years too soon. In 1955 two young cleaners were at the sand furnace, going through the usual ritual of practising their ability with the shovel, when they realised that they had overdone it. The fire was completely blacked out, with not a flame or a spark in sight, and thinking that they would be in trouble, one of them, Dave Nickless, went to the stores for a bucket of paraffin because the older cleaner, whose name was Pearce, had asked him to get it. When Pearce got the paraffin he threw the bucketful into the dead fire and in seconds they were both enveloped in a thick cloud of white vapour. As they were in a confined space, they couldn't see their way out. Dave Nickless, who told me about it afterwards, said that he heard Pearce fumbling with a box of matches, and the next thing that happened was a tremendous explosion that flung both of them back on to the heap of coal behind them. They had badly singed hair, eyebrows and eyelashes. Of course, the furnace fire was not out and they had been taught a lesson that remained with them. Although Dave Nickless later left the railway, he became a member of my family when he married my daughter, Wendy, and I have three sturdy grandsons who have all had rides in the cab with me.

Having moved from Guildford to Reading in September 1937, I was booked out firing on odd occasions, mostly on the yard shunting engines. I still have vivid memories while on those yard duties, one of which includes watching the early services to Waterloo leaving the old Southern Region station; these usually comprised eight coaches headed by one of Stirling's Class F1 locomotives. The yard was about 200 yards from the station and by the time the train reached us, a sheer column of fire was being emitted from the chimney. I used to wonder how the fireman kept time with that sort of hammering, but learnt later that the old Class F1s used to thrive on a good hiding and, really, with the load, the gradient and the sharp timing, it was the way they had to be worked. The Class F1s had driving wheels of a little under 7ft., and were the passenger engines for the Waterloo and Redhill road at that time. From memory I remember Nos. 1002, 1042, 1043, 1062, 1078, 1079, 1110, 1140, 1182, 1183, 1195, 1205. Many times I have stood on Crowthorne Station waiting for the last train to go to Reading, and it was easy to listen and hear the train leaving Sandhurst about 3½ to 4 miles away. First the two white lights over the front buffer beam could be seen and, as the train got nearer, a dull red glow at the bottom of the smokebox. The smokebox doors, with just a central locking key, used to warp slighty and draw air, and with a wall of hot ashes in the smokebox, it became a fire against the smokebox door, making the lower third of the door red hot.

On Christmas Eve 1937, which I believe was a Saturday, I was on duty with Driver Bob Ward, with whom I was on the station shunting engines until 1a.m. when we 'came to shed'. We had to dispose of the engine and then dispose of two others, which meant cleaning fires, smokeboxes and ashpans. I had some help from my mate, but it was 4.15a.m. by the time I had finished. My driver went home, and I was hoping that the driver of the 5a.m. van train to Redhill would drop me off at Crowthorne. It was Driver Fred Marshall, and he said

'Yes, it's Christmas Day, you haven't got a train until 10a.m.'. I sat in the messroom for ten minutes and Charlie Rolfe, the steam raiser, who was the only man in charge, came in and said 'Will you go with Fred Marshall and work the van train to Redhill, the fireman hasn't come in yet and he's due off the shed in ten minutes.' I said 'My mate has booked me off duty and I'm not officially here.' I then went and talked to the driver who explained that Bill Kirke would be in trouble if the train was cancelled, so I decided to go, as Bill Kirke was also a cleaner who was booked out for firing, although three years senior to me.

The engine was No. 1802, a tender engine that had originally been a 'River' class tank, and one of the engines that was involved in the Sevenoaks disaster of 1927. I think they were converted due to the high centre of gravity of the engines as tanks, which was considered partly to blame for the accident. Should anyone like to check, I believe 1937 was a white Christmas, and I had never seen the Redhill road until that time, but I shall always remember the lovely picture-postcard scene of the hills around Dorking covered with snow. We had relief on arrival at Redhill, and caught a train back to Reading at around 9am. Driver Marshall showed Bill Kirke as his fireman for the duty, and this gentleman had arrived for work ten minutes after we had left Reading, and the next week Bill Kirke paid me 9s. 0d. for the overtime I had worked for him. Local management were involved in squaring up what had occurred, and they should have booked a cover man on at 4a.m., so they worked out the amount Bill Kirke had to pay me — that was the way things were then.

Into 1938, and I was out firing quite a bit. There was extra ballast working for building electric sub-stations and for putting down the third rail over the Waterloo road, so twelve drivers had to be trained to be electric train drivers at Reading — all making more work.

Another type of traffic that gave us extra work at Reading was horse-box specials. Before the days of the motor horse-box, it was common during big race meetings at Ascot, Sandown, Kempton, Hurst Park or Epsom, to see as many as twenty boxes rolling down the bank from the many racing stables in Berkshire. The bottom of the old bank at Reading was where the interchange of traffic took place on the 'up' road and was also the location of Reading (Southern) Junction box, where the attaching and detaching of engines took place under the eye of the signalman. One ritual which had to take place when the Southern engine was on the front, was pulling the wires on the brake cylinders of all vehicles, this being because the GWR engines worked on 25in. of vacuum, and the Southern engines at 21in., all vacuum in the train being destroyed and a new brake created.

During July 1938 I was booked on a horse-box special with Driver George Nash. To my knowledge this man was unique in one respect, in that he had been sent to pass the driving exam during 1933 and failed the eyesight test, thus losing his job at about forty years of age. He was put back in the shed on one of the dirtiest of jobs, as a boiler washer, but he persevered with his eyes and looked after them so that he was able to take a retest in 1937 and get his job back. He stayed on the main line until 1963 when he retired, passing all eyesight tests as required. We worked ten horse-boxes to Esher for Sandown Park Races, going via the Western Curve at Virginia Water. There was a special race platform at Esher at the time, and after the horses were unloaded the boxes were shunted to the sidings, and we came light engine to Reading. One of the horses we took, which won the Eclipse Stakes — a very valuable race — that day, was called Pasch. The horse was trained by Fred Darling, and ridden by Gordon Richards.

The engine that day was Chatham Class R1 0-4-4 tank No. 1709, designed by Wainwright; these were useful little engines with a sensible reversing wheel. Reading had an allocation of five, and they did some useful work. One duty started with the 6.50a.m. service to Ash with six coaches and then back to Reading, and two trips to Virginia Water and back. There was a similar duty which finished with the last connection from London, which started from Virginia Water. I have always felt that a serious error of judgement was made by the Management when it was decided to close the Western Curve. It couldn't have been more than 150 yards from junction to junction, and the cost of maintenance must have been minimal compared with the cost of booking extra men on duty for shunting and plugging crossover points, to get from the 'up' Reading line to the 'down' Chertsey line or vice versa. The working of the junction could easily have been slotted into the control of Feltham panel box.

Over the past fifteen years I have lost count of the number of times I have been required to work the Reading service, both 'up' and 'down', via the main line and Virginia Water because of fires on the track, derailments, bodies on the line, interference with the electric rail, bomb scares etc. As recently as September and October 1982 we were required to conduct Redhill and Reading Western Region men on the Gatwick service via Byfleet Junction and Woking, still going through the same serious delays at Virginia Water. With the starting of the electric service on 2nd January

18

1939, the steam work to Waterloo would be finished, and the danger signals were out for the cleaners with subsequent loss of work. In November 1938 we were informed that twelve of us would be redundant; five were to go to Basingstoke, four to Redhill and three to Feltham. The choice of depot was to go to the senior men downwards, with the youngest having to take what was left. I came third in seniority and while the two senior cleaners chose Basingstoke, I opted for Feltham, along with Gordon Thorpe and Jack Hockley, the two cleaners who immediately followed me in seniority. We took up our jobs as cleaners at Feltham on 2nd January 1939.

At Feltham there were about eighty cleaners working three shifts; 8a.m. until 4p.m., 4p.m. until midnight and midnight until 8a.m. All engines had to be properly cleaned before they left the depot and, as at Guildford, each man in a gang of ten was responsible for his own particular part of the engine. Engines that went off the shed at 1a.m., and every twenty minutes or so through the early hours of the morning, would often be returning between 9a.m., 10a.m. and 11a.m., and it was not uncommon for the Depot Manager, Mr Oxley, to go out on to the disposal pits when the engines returned and examine the underneath of a Stephenson's link motion engine. Big ends, small ends, foreway and backway eccentrics and all linkages had to be shining and clean, otherwise the cleaner responsible was traced and Mr Oxley would 'tear him off a strip' the next time that cleaner was on daywork. Running his fingers up the back of wheel spokes, if the Governor picked up any oil or grease, a carpeting for the cleaner responsible was ensured.

Within a few weeks I began to have the good fortune to be booked out as a fireman two or three times a week, and by the beginning of April 1939 I was on firing duties most of the time. The work was either on the west end shunter with Adams 'Jumbo' engines or the Datchet or Kingston shunter, with a Class 700 'Black Motor' or a Class 137 'Small Hopper' in charge. The 'Jumbo' engines ensured the fireman was kept busy, as the steam brake for shunting was on the fireman's side, so that either he watched the shunter and operated the steam brake, or he stayed the other side of the footplate and manhandled the pole reverser backwards and forwards on the instructions of the driver. As most of the drivers were failed main line men with various disabilities, the fireman generally operated the reverser. With the fire to attend to as well, we always went home with aching arms and back. The 'Black Motor' locomotives on the Datchet shunter were nice engines, but very cold in the winter with no cab doors, just a chain to stop you falling out, which left two wide gaps both side of the cab.

Before leaving the 'Black Motor' engines I must say that years later, both as a fireman and driver, I worked many excursion trains from Reading, via Peasmarsh Junction, over the pretty Cranleigh road to Horsham, for Bognor Regis, Littlehampton and other Sussex resorts, always with ten or eleven coaches and stopping at most stations from Reading to Guildford. The 'Black Motor' locomotives replaced the Class F1s on these trains, and performed the job more comfortably, although they in turn were very much outshone by the Class Q1 Austerity engines on the same jobs.

I had about three weeks working with the same driver on Feltham Hump. We always had one of the big Class G16 4-8-0 tanks of which there were four, — Nos. 493 to 496 inclusive, — built especially for the job of moving a long heavy train slowly towards and up the incline of the hump, where the wagons were uncoupled so that they would run into their required reception or departure siding; the hump signalman operating the points. The number of the siding for the next batch of wagons was chalked on the rear vehicle of the batch running over the hump — simple, but very effective.

My elder brother Jack, who had just retained his position as a cleaner at Guildford in September 1937, was still only cleaning — in fact, men who were six to eight years senior to him were also cleaning all the time. This meant that I was going home on pay days with never less than £3 to £4 while my brother, who was almost two years senior to me, was on 6s .0d. a day which was £1 16s. 0d. a week before stoppages. The cleaners I had left behind at Guildford knew of this situation, so a letter was written to Mr E. S. Moore, the Chief Motive Power Superintendent, complaining that junior cleaners at Feltham were regularly performing firing duties. Seniority was very strictly upheld on the Southern Region and, as a result of the complaint, the cleaners at Guildford were informed by E. S. Moore that if they applied to move to Feltham as cleaners, with the object of performing firing duties, up to ten of them would receive favourable consideration; ten cleaners made the move towards the end of April 1939, my brother being one of them. As I was aware of the situation, I contacted the two chaps I had moved from Reading with and we applied for a move back to Reading, returning on the same day as the cleaners moved from Guildford to Feltham. Mr E. S. Moore was a much respected man who would not tolerate liars, but if you told him the truth he was a fair man. He was Motive Power Foreman at Bognor in 1916, and had won a 'Blue' in the Cambridge boat around 1896/7. I had a chat to Fred Wilson an ex-Reading driver, who is 82 years of age and moved to Reading in 1942 as a driver, and he told me that he was office boy to E. S. Moore during

1916, and every day at 12.30p.m., Mr Moore left the depot, bought a small loaf at the bakery on the corner, half a pound of cheese at the grocers next door, went back to the locomotive shed, took a large knife from his pocket and ate the lot. This was his lunch everyday without fail. He later retired, and lived until well into his nineties at Weybridge.

Fred Wilson claims that he was probably the only engine cleaner to drive a main line electric train. Because steam drivers at Bognor would not take the job on electric trains unless it was regular, it became necessary to pass some firemen to act as drivers to cover holidays and sickness. Fred Wilson was one of the men who were passed and trained on electric traction; after a few months Bognor Depot lost three duties and F. Wilson lost his job as fireman, and was put back as a cleaner. On his first day back cleaning, a driver at Littlehampton went sick, and the only person available to cover the duty was Fred Wilson, so the foreman sent him to work the 6.30p.m. service from Littlehampton to London and back, and he duly obliged. Thus he went from cleaner to driver on the same day and as this was in 1938, he did have 22 years of service.

CHAPTER TWO

Reading — The Vital Wartime Junction

Back at Reading, in early May 1939, things had not altered much. No. 1639 of the crack U class was still at the depot, this being the engine that worked the 8.30a.m. Reading to Oxford train and returned with the 'Continental' from Oxford to Redhill. This train started at Birkenhead in one direction and worked to Dover with portions for Bournemouth and various Sussex resorts such as Brighton, with also a portion for Canterbury, Folkstone and other Kent resorts. The 'up' service started from Dover and collected portions en route, leaving Redhill with nine coaches, with three more coaches from Bournemouth being attached at Guildford.

No. 1639 had one unusual feature; instead of one small vacuum-brake ejector on the brake equipment, another small ejector valve was fitted just below the original valve, which was expected to assist in maintaining 21in. vacuum in the event of a fall in steam pressure. I never knew it to be used as No. 1639, like all of her breed, was a good steamer. I was still getting plenty of firing duties, generally four days as a fireman and two days as a cleaner while the Ascot Races in June, excursion traffic and holidays and sickness to be covered, ensured that I was more or less a regular fireman. With the outbreak of war, on 3rd September 1939, every footplateman was instructed to sign on the first Sunday with the same man that they worked with on the Saturday.

At a fair in Crowthorne, on 15th June 1939, I met the girl I knew I would marry, Kathleen, a Welsh girl from Abertillery, who had taken a job as housemaid in Wellington College. Together we brought up four children, two boys and two girls.

From the start of World War II I seemed to be booked with one particular driver, who was actually a senior fireman passed to act as a driver. Dick Lester had started as a cleaner at Reading in 1915 and knew all the routes from Reading, by the Western Region to Oxford or Basingstoke, Feltham, Nine Elms, Willesden, the main line from Basingstoke to Waterloo and also Alton to Waterloo via Aldershot.

Merstham, Redhill, the Portsmouth line to Haslemere and the single line to Christ's Hospital and Horsham via Peasmarsh Junction were also on his route card. The work we performed together was of great help to me, and when I passed for driving, in 1949, my own route card was similar. I learnt from Dick Lester the beautiful flavour of bacon and eggs cooked on the firing shovel, bread and cheese toasted on the ring of the firebox and, best of all, in my opinion, a nice bloater wrapped in tissue paper, which was then placed against the boiler lagging behind the water-gauge column. On a trip to Redhill, if the fish was turned at Guildford, it was, for me, a delicacy no chef could equal.

In the winter of 1939, long hours on duty for footplatemen became commonplace. The vast increase in the movement of freight traffic often caused the block to go on at large marshalling yards, and the use of 'permissive block' was a regular occurrence. This system allowed trains to follow each other for several miles, through what was known as a goods loop, with each driver stopping just short of the train in front and all moving forward in stages as the leading train was signalled back out on to the main line. By this means you had to wait and take your turn, and there was nothing you could do about it. During this period my elder brother was called up and, being a keen motor cycle enthusiast, he joined the Royal Army Service Corps and became a dispatch rider, going to France with the British Expeditionary Forces in October 1939.

All railwaymen were being called up as their turn came, with most of them going into the Railway Operating Department of the Army and receiving their training at Longmore, on the military railway at Bordon in Hampshire. The 'Continental' from Birkenhead then became known as the 'Leave Train', and ran from Ashford in Kent through to Newcastle. It was still routed via Redhill and Reading, and stopped at the main stations via Birmingham, Derby, Sheffield and York. Reading gained more work from this, this service relieving Redhill men at Reading and working through to Banbury where it arrived at about 1.30p.m. After necessary loco duties at Banbury, we worked the return trains, ex-Newcastle, back to Reading at about 3.00p.m., where another pair of Reading men relieved us, and worked through to Redhill. It was always a three cylinder Class U1 locomotive on this duty, usually No. 1892, 1894 or 1897 which were Redhill engines. I never considered these engines to be as good as the Class U locomotives Nos. 1610 and upwards, because although they were running to the same timing as the 'Castle' class engines of the GWR they managed it on the comparatively level road to Oxford, but the stop at Heyford and the sharp climb out of the station, together with the steady climb the rest of the way to Banbury, invariably caused struggle, with the water being well down the glass. The engine was always coaled with Betteshangar, from another Kent colliery, but as good as Welsh coal was on steam locomotives, it was generally agreed, by those of us who used it, that Betteshangar surpassed it. It had all the qualities of Welsh coal, but it would never let you down on a 'knob up' as Welsh coal sometimes did. A 'knob up' was frowned on by any ex-L&SWR driver, probably with good reason because the fire-bars of their engines were closer together. Dugald Drummond, their main locomotive designer, was a Scot, and paid close attention to economy and the consumption of fuel with, it must be admitted, very good results.

The system for a 'knob up' was to have a nice hot body of fire spread thinly over the firebox. Hand-picked fist sized lumps were then thrown right to the front of the box, against the tube plate, until the firebox was solid to the brick-arch from front to back; there had to be no gaps anywhere, but the lumps could get progressively larger once the brick-arch was cleared. The back corners of the firebox were then packed solid until no more coal could be thrown in, and the baffle plate was then replaced. Ash pan dampers were always left open during this operation, which took about one hour to complete, and well over a ton of coal was in the firebox when the job was finished. I have never been let down by a firebox full of Betteshangar coal; with both coals, a flickering yellow flame was assurance that everything was all right but you had to look out for blue flames, and if you saw any you were going to be in trouble for steam — we only ever saw a blue flame with Welsh coal. With a twelve coach train from Banbury to Reading there was no need to pick up the shovel, and the engine was handed over to the other crew with a lovely red hot box of fire and a tender to shovel from, which was fully coaled for the heavy trip to Redhill.

At the commencement of World War II all engines had been fitted with black-out sheets, this entailed extra fittings on the tenders and slim metal rods along both sides of the engine, from the tender to the front of the cab inside the footplate. The main sheet was fixed on hooks, under the cab roof on the inside, and stretched well back into the tender to metal supports where it was tied by ropes attached to the sheets. The side-sheets were tied back into the tender during daylight, and were pulled along the rail like a curtain at dusk. They were filthy heavy sheets of a sort of asphalt material, cerainly a time-wasting nuisance but, of course, very necessary. They made footplate work far more difficult, particularly when working heavy trains during darkness.

What later became a far more serious problem was the shortage of tools, including lamps. Most engines were superheated which necessitated a sight-feed lubricator in the cab, the oil being carried by steam to the internal movement of the valves and pistons. The lubricator filling plug required a ¾ in. spanner and they became very scarce; it is possible that because of this many men kept their own spanner in their locker, which only served to increase the shortage. The same thing applied to the ⅞ in. spanner, which was required to release and secure the nuts on the smokebox door so that the smokebox could be regularly cleared of ashes.

Handbrushes, shovels, buckets, fire-irons, gauge lamps and head and tail lamps also became short, until a stage was reached when we did not dare leave the footplate of an engine that we had prepared or we would have lost the tools that we had diligently collected. Even then, occasions arose when you could leave a locomotive depot in the dark and when you set back on to your train, and went to remove your tail lamp from the tender, it was missing as some fool had taken it as you started to move off the shed. Along with many other men I drew the attention of the management to the dangers, until eventually a system was developed whereby all engines were fully tooled, with chains and locks being supplied, and when an engine was left at a locomotive shed, it was the fireman's duty to lock all tools away and then hand the keys into the stores. The next pair of men required to work on the engine would then ask for the keys at commencement of their duty.

On Wednesday, 29th May 1940 I worked a normal Reading duty, starting with the 9.03a.m. passenger train to Redhill and returning with the 1.31p.m. Redhill to Reading service, the engine being Class F1 No. 1110. When we arrived at Redhill Locomotive Depot we were told that our return working was cancelled, and that we would be working a special train back to Reading. Another pair of Reading men, who had worked the 8.20a.m. service from Reading and were due to work the 12.31p.m. train back to Reading, were given similar instructions. They also had Class F1 locomotive, No. 1079. I was on the footplate of No. 1079 talking to the fireman when their train ran into Redhill from the Tonbridge line and, to our surprise, it was an eleven coach train. Our own train followed in about twenty minutes, also comprised of eleven coaches. I will not name my driver, for he is no longer with us, but of all the ex-SECR drivers who hated anything to do with the L&SWR he was by far the worst. He called Drummond's engines 'rice pudding engines', and whenever he had to work on one he claimed he was a 'high-bred man on a low-bred horse'.

His problem on the day in question was that the driver on the previous train, Bill Chown, was an ex-L&SWR driver, and my driver was wondering if the other driver would attempt to climb the bank away from Guildford with the small four-coupled Class F1 locomotive, or if he would stop at Guildford for an assisting engine. He asked my opinion and I said that it might be possible, given a good run through platform 8 at Guildford, but not otherwise. What worried my mate was the indignity he would suffer if the ex-L&SWR driver in front, on the ex-SECR engine, went through without assistance, but we decided to stop at Guildford for an assisting engine. Although we went through Dorking at speed, by the time the top of the long climb up Dorking Bank was reached we were all out and barely moving, although the engine was steaming well. This was enough to convince my driver to put a note off at Chilworth signal box requesting assistance from Guildford, and he was very pleased to learn at Guildford that the train in front had stopped for an assisting engine. As I recall it was an Adams 'Jubilee' class engine, No. 546, that was coupled to the front of us and after Pinks Hill Bank had been mastered, with both engines working hard, my mate set about getting to Reading as fast as possible.

With the gradual descent from Ash Junction to Sandhurst, and further favourable conditions from Crowthorne to Reading, we completed the journey in just under thirty minutes. We uncoupled at Reading Junction and dropped into Reading Yard, while the GWR 'Hall' class locomotive coupled up to the train and worked it away. While standing in Reading Yard I noticed that a left-hand side tender box of the 'Jubilee' engine was smoking badly and on examination revealed that the journal was melted out. This amused my mate, as the speed of the ex-SECR engine had caused the ex-L&SWR engine to run hot; he went home happy. The passengers on those two trains were some of the 47,000 British troops lifted off the beaches at Dunkirk that day although we didn't know that at the time, of course, and it was several weeks afterwards that what really had happened was made known. It is history now that for the next few days — Thursday, 30th May (54,000), Friday, 31st May (68,000), Saturday, 1st June (64,000), Sunday, 2nd June (26,000), Monday, 3rd June and Tuesday, 4th June — (27,000 each day) all troops escaping from Dunkirk and surrounding beaches, and the railwaymen of all grades played their part in clearing the British ports.

All normal services from Reading to Tonbridge were cancelled, the vital requirement being empty passenger stock, so we all signed on with the same driver and left the locomotive shed in turn to tie on to the next lot of stock which came down the bank from the GWR, worked to Redhill, and waited for the next available trainload of troops to come up from the coast. Most of the time the troops were in a bad way, many with just a blanket to cover themselves, but there was only one thing they ever asked of us and that was to notify someone that they were safe. I collected many pieces of paper from them with just a name, address and signature, and the driver I was with agreed to share them and post a note to the address, together with a note of our own, explaining that they were safe in this country.

Redhill Locomotive Depot was comparatively small, and on the Thursday it was obvious that more engines were converging on the shed than could adequately be coped with. Engines were sent from the station but not being able to enter the depot were shunted behind Earlswood signal box to await their turn. Because of this, the average time from leaving Reading with empty stock and returning with troops was twelve to fourteen hours. Of course, Ashford and Tonbridge engines were also being dealt with.

My girlfriend had one Sunday off a fortnight, from 2p.m. until 10p.m. and Sunday, 2nd June was her day off. With this in mind I asked a fireman, who was on at 2a.m., if he would change turns with me so that I took his turn on Sunday 2nd and he came on at 9a.m. on my duty. He readily agreed, as it gave him a night in bed, but in my case it meant signing on again after a short rest but no-one bothered about that. I finished work at 9p.m. on Saturday, 1st June, got out of bed at 1a.m. on Sunday and cycled from Crowthorne to Reading. After cleaning the fires on a couple of engines we were instructed to work the 6a.m. Reading to Guildford workman's special, with Class C2X Brighton 'Vulcan'. Waiting orders at Guildford, the foreman instructed us to relieve the crew on the next train of empty stock for Redhill, so we took over on engine No. 1410 at 9.45a.m., with an eleven coach train. The engine was one of a small batch of Class N Maunsell-designed locomotives, on which the driver worked from the left side of the engine and the fireman on the right. It was a long laborious crawl from signal to signal all the way to Redhill, arriving there at 1p.m. Redhill was more choked than ever, and we finished up with fourteen other engines behind Earlswood signal box at about 2.30p.m. and moved out to the locomotive engine line at 6p.m.

The date with my girlfriend was now looking a bit sick, and we eventually set back on to a twelve coach train a 9.45p.m., but couldn't get away from Redhill until 10.30p.m., still waiting our turn behind other trains. The troops were all French soldiers, the train being for Southampton so that they could get back to France as quickly as possible, so we ran round our train at Woking and faced the trip down the main line tender first. We informed the authorities that we would be almost out of coal at Basingstoke, and left Woking at 1a.m., taking an hour to get to Basingstoke. I had eaten my last sandwich at Guildford that morning and by now we were both starving, so when we came off the train at Basingstoke and went to the locomotive shed, we soon disposed of a couple of cheese rolls each. We ran light from Basingtoke to Reading, No. 1410 proving to be a good engine, but I was dead tired when we reached Reading Shed at 3.40a.m., after 25½ hours on duty. After forty years of marriage, my wife still tells me I stood her up that day. When I next saw Les Beard, the fireman who I had changed turns with, I learnt that he had stayed spare at Reading and finished at 4.30p.m.

At around this time we were informed that my brother had been injured in a motor-cycle accident in France, and had been moved to Alder Hey Hospital, Liverpool, a few days before the Dunkirk evacuation. During late August and September a good many air battles took place in the skies around Redhill, and I counted nine parachutes drifting downwards on one occasion. A German Heinkel 111 came down alongside the line, between Deepdene and Betchworth, and struggling up Dorking Bank one afternoon I saw a Hurricane fighter, losing height rapidly, which crash-landed into a clump of trees about 100 yards from the line.

Whilst working the 8.33p.m. Redhill to Reading service one night, with Driver Wally Selves, I was standing on a Class F1 locomotive and was peering into the darkness, looking for Betchworth distant signal, when suddenly the engine gave a terrific lurch to the left and I thought we were going over. We later reported the incident to the signalman at Betchworth, who contacted a railwayman living at the nearby Brockham Crossing and asked him to examine the track. He reported that a bomb had exploded in the cess on the left of the 'down' line, which had resulted in blowing out the ballast from the left side rail. We learnt later from the ganger that, for a distance of 10 yards, the sleepers on the left side were suspended a yard in the air and that, in his opinion, it was the 7ft. driving wheels of the Class F1 engine which kept us on the rails. The road was closed for several hours, while the track was repaired, and the last train, the 9.33p.m. Redhill to Reading working was re-routed via Horsham, Christ's Hospital and Peasmarsh Junction to Guildford.

Towards the end of 1940 Reading gained four Class U engines, losing the three Chatham tanks Nos. 1699, 1708, and 1709. Two of the Class U locomotives, Nos. 1610 and 1611 came from Guildford while Nos. 1621 and 1627 came from somewhere in the West of England. The bigger engines were required for the important freight and passenger special work which was coming through Reading, and it was becoming increasingly obvious that the junction was of vital importance for traffic from the North of England and the Midlands to the south, avoiding London. The Redhill line via Guildford was the important connecting link.

The two shunting yards at Reading (Southern Railway) were working 24 hours a day, and traffic flow was of such volume that it was decided to put a controller on each shift to take charge of the movements between the two regions. The interchange of traffic, from Southern Railway to Great Western Railway could only take place when a GWR engine came down the bank for a train, which was then hauled on to the 'up' SR line by the yard shunting engine. The GWR engine then coupled to the other end and worked away, mostly up the bank but sometimes through the tunnel and up the bank the other side, which connected with the 'up' and 'down' goods loops of Reading (GWR). What are now the two electric sidings at Reading were of greater extent, and belonged to the GWR. This meant that traffic for the Southern Railway was stabled there, and as soon as it was moved by the Southern yard shunter, another train soon took its place.

There were many times when the Southern yards held two or three trains ready for the GWR, but could not get them moved which resulted in restricting the shunting ability in the yards. After several incidents, when the yard virtually came to a standstill, one controller decided to do something about it. Laurie Cox gave the GWR an ultimatum that in future it was to be a train for a train, and nothing would be moved from Reading Junction to Reading Yard unless a train was taken from Reading Yard to the GWR. After it became obvious that he meant what he said, the GWR accepted the situation and things seemed to work more freely between the two regions. What is much more important, the disagreement was instrumental in fostering the first plans for the building of Reading Spur, or New Junction as it is now known.

Many years later, some time in the 1960s when Laurie Cox was stationmaster at Waterloo, I met him on the concourse and said 'Good morning Sir'. 'Look here Rowee', he said, 'If Laurie was good enough at Reading Yard, it's good enough here at Waterloo'. I grinned at him and said 'I'm not necessarily addressing you as Sir, but simply showing respect for the position you hold'. 'Oh that's all right then', he said. Laurie was a great character, and just about the most efficient railwayman I ever met. I know of no station-master of recent years who could have held a candle to him, — a man who started on the railways as a lamp boy at the age of fourteen.

A system was evolved, during World War II, of making the best and quickest use of empty freight wagons by a means of pooling. If Reading Yard had forty or more empties, a special train ran to where the empties were required and if Ascot Gasworks, Bracknell and Wokingham had forty or fifty empties between them, a special engine sorted them out, formed a train and worked away. These trains were known as pool trains, and the name stuck for many years after the war.

On Sunday, 29th December 1940 I signed on at 3p.m., again with Dick Lester, and we worked a pool train for Willesden from Wokingham with engine No. 1611. At Brentford there was another engine waiting, crewed by Feltham men, and the man in charge asked us to come off and go light engine to Nine Elms Yard, to work an urgently required train of gas coal to Reading Gasworks. On our journey we were stopped at Barnes and informed that a 'red warning' was in force, although this was quite common and meant that German bombers had crossed the coast and were in the area.

We were in Nine Elms Locomotive Shed at about 6.30p.m., and had just taken coal when there was a dull thud. About 30 yards away there was a brilliant glow like a huge sparkler, throwing red hot metal in a radius of about 8 yards, the cause being an incendiary bomb, although I was not aware of this at the time. As we moved out of the shed, just after 7p.m., I looked towards Waterloo and every-thing seemed to be burning; looking to the right of Waterloo the sky seemed to be alight all round to London Bridge, and to the left and behind Waterloo all we could see was flames. We coupled up to our train in Nine Elms Yard, and I made sure I had my tin hat on when I removed the tail lamp from the tender. The guard, Fred Challis of Reading, climbed on the engine to inform my mate of the load and said he had just left the yard signal box, where he had been waiting for us, and there was a message that several trains were on fire at Waterloo. As we pulled up through Queen's Road Station, there were fires burning to the left and right, in Battersea and Clapham and more again at Wandsworth. It was a sickening experience, as we could still see the glow in the sky from the Ascot area. We learnt later that the city had been practically gutted by fire.

Things were getting steadily worse on the footplate throughout 1941. Engines were often coaled with coke and straw and because skilled fitters were being called up, serious steam blows were commonplace, and the general standard of upkeep on locomotives had declined. Engines had to be taken out of servies, sometimes with only one injector working, or a train would be cancelled with the same conditions applying generally throughout the country. Because the main theatre of war for the Army was in North Africa, soldiers who had some railway experience were sent to ride on engines to assist the young firemen that were being taken on as cleaners, but were used as fireman almost at once to replace experienced men who were being called up. It wasn't a successful idea, as three men on the footplate was never comfortable and the soldiers were seldom conversant with the engines.

Early in 1941 I received my calling up papers, and I was to travel to Chester three weeks later, but three days before I was due to go the shedmaster, Mr Collins, called me into his office and showed me official papers cancelling my call up. I argued about it and threatened to go anyway, but he explained that I now came under the Essential Works Order and that I would have to do as I was told. I found out later that it was a top Government decision and, looking back, it made sense because the railways retained their experienced firemen and, where possible, available fitters etc. were also sent back to railway duties. My elder brother, after convalescing, was also sent back to footplate duties at Feltham.

Towards the end of 1940 my brother George (known as 'Rusty' because of his red hair) started at Reading as a cleaner, being booked out as a fireman early in 1941. He soon settled into the job, and was popular because of his desire to learn the mechanics of steam locomotion and the vacuum-brake. He soon mastered the relationship of side rods to big ends and eccentrics, thereby knowing which ports were open to steam, which were closed and which way the valves would move with the reverser in a given position. He was, in fact, a capable lecturer at the mutual improvement classes by the time he was eighteen years of age but he had the misfortune to be overtaken by diabetes when he was getting near to passing for driving duties in 1948. Rusty performed duties as a shed engineman's mate until 1956, when he passed a clerical exam and moved to Feltham. He was, for many years, the motive power list clerk at Nine Elms, moving to Waterloo as chief list clerk in 1967 at the closure of Nine Elms Shed, and recently moved to Feltham as chief clerk. Top drivers at Nine Elms have told me that when they first had Bulleid's Pacifics, and arguments took place about the relationship of the valves and pistons of the middle engine to that of the outside engines, brother George could always sort it out for them. As far as my brother's experiences as a fireman are concerned two instances come to mind, both occurring during World War II.

Freight trains of petrol and ammunition were invariably well over the load for one Class U engine, so double-heading was a regular feature during night duties over the Redhill road. On this occasion, I was firing to a Class U engine with Driver Walt Allen while my brother was on the Class F1 locomotive with Driver George Powell, the Class F1 being in the lead. Our train comprised 34 large tanks of petrol which were heavy, and once Shalford distant signal was spotted as 'clear' both drivers set about getting a run up through Chilworth and the long climb up Shere Heath. As the train was moving on to the straight after the sharp curve beyond Chilworth, we seemed to be going slower and slower, and both drivers were working the engines harder. I looked back along the train, mainly to see that all the train and the brake van were following round the curve, and immediately noticed the guard waving a red light from side to side. At the same time, I could also see why. An axlebox on one of the petrol tanks was alight, and it was little wonder the guard had screwed his brake hard on. I shouted to my mate at once and attracted my brother's attention with the whistle, and as the two drivers closed the regulators the train came to a stand. Rusty and I then ran back with our firing shovels and threw sandy soil from the lineside on to the burning axlebox, quickly bringing it under control. After a chat with the guard it was agreed that we should proceed very slowly to Gomshall, where the defective tank could be stood off. We had no trouble identifying it as smoke was pouring from it again, but it was safely shunted into the siding, under the watchful eye of the signalman, and we all went on our way thinking it could have been a lot worse.

The other incident concerning my brother occurred when he had been on duty for over twelve hours, and had shovelled a lot of coal. He was with Driver Bob Sawyer, and they were shunted inside at Bracknell with an ambulance train at about 2a.m. Rusty was dead tired, and his mate suggested that he should go and get his head down in the train, and he would give him a call when it was time to move. He climbed into the train, lay down on the floor and was fast asleep in minutes, not waking until about 6a.m. when it was daylight. He climbed back on to the engine and there was a look of sheer panic on his driver's face. 'Whats's happened mate?' asked the driver, 'Your face is covered in blood'. Rusty assured him that he was all right, and when they looked in the train they realised what had happened. He had slept in the mortuary of the ambulance train! Perhaps it was just as well he woke up when he did because the cleaners were on duty at 6a.m., and their first job was to clean out the train.

Crowthorne C. E. School
Berkshire
April 16th 1934

The Locomotive Running Superintendent.
Waterloo Station
S. E. I.

Dear Sir

With reference to your enquiry, I have great pleasure in recommending James Alfred Rowe, formerly a scholar under my charge.
I have known him for nearly 12 years.
He made satisfactory progress at school.
He is intelligent, strong and industrious, honest and reliable.
I feel sure he is a suitable candidate for the employment he seeks.
[His father & older brother are both employed by the Southern Railway Company]

Yours faithfully
A. C. Goodband M.R.S.T.
Head Master.

This character reference from my schoolmaster was required before the Southern Railway would consider employing me in the Motive

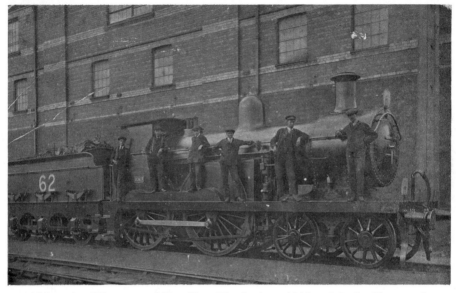

(Above): The rear of Reading Shed, circa 1918, with the East main signal box in the background.

(Below): Reading Southern and Great Western stations, circa 1865. The building on the left is the old Great Western Hotel, now used as offices.

(Berkshire County Library)

(Above): An original Stirling Class F1, No. 194, photographed while passing Folkestone Junction. These locomotives were known affectionately by the men as 'Chaffcutters'.

(Below): This scene is believed to be between Merstham and Redhill, with Class C goods locomotive No. 580 providing the motive power.

(Above): Reading Southern Shed during the early 1930s, with Class M7 No. 251 on the left and Class F1 No. 1183 on the right.

(Below): 'Schools' class, No. 30926 *Repton.*

(Above): Class U 2-6-0 No. 1631, pictured at Reading while stopped for repairs, with a Western Region main box to the rear of the engine's tender.

(Below): No. 30519 on the new pit at Reading Locomotive Depot.

(Above): Class E superheated 'Coppertop' No. 1587 sits on the middle road at the front of Reading Southern Shed, with a Urie 4-6-2T in the background.

(Below): A graceful Class T9 4-4-0, No. 30718, possibly at Redhill Depot.

(Above): Maunsell Class A, No. 30839 at Bracknell, in July 1965.

(Below): The 'down' road at Ascot.

(Above): Standard Class 5 No. 73119, pictured at Nine Elms on 23rd July 1958.

(Below): On 23rd October 1960, Class 4 2-6-4T No. 80151 waits at Redhill.

Sometime during 1941 a siding was put in which went off to the left of the 'up' road, about half-way up the incline coming out of the junction with the GWR at Reading. The siding then continued to run parallel with the 'up' Southern line for about 200 yards to some buffer stops. To the left of the siding, on the GWR side, was a deep valley which went down for about 45 yards and levelled out at the bottom for 15 yards, then rising fairly steeply up to the GWR 'down' main line. The latter was a natural valley, which extended almost to the River Kennet, with the bank on the GWR main line side being at a higher elevation than the bank on the Southern side, by about 15 yards. The new siding was known as 'Dunkirk Siding', and the name stuck with it well into the 1970s. As soon as the siding was finished three train loads of chalk ran every day from Merstham to Reading, stopped half-way up the bank in Reading Junction and were then propelled back up into Dunkirk Siding. The load was always 26 drop side trucks, and gangs were on hand to shovel the chalk out of the wagons straight into the valley between the two railways.

Three small goods engines became additions to Reading motive power during this period, these locomotives always working 26 empties to Merstham and returning with a train load of chalk. One was an ex-Brighton 'Vulcan', No. 32523, while the other two were ex-SECR Class C goods engines, Nos. 1287 and 1317. All three engines were 0-6-0, and I fired to all three on these chalk trains many times. I preferred the Class C engines, mainly because they were more comfortable to work on and the injectors were more reliable. The 'Vulcan' steamed just as freely as the Class Cs but the Westinghouse brake pump was never reliable, and seldom was a trip completed without the driver or fireman going round the framings with a spanner to give the donkey pump a couple of clouts to make it work. With 26 loaded trucks both classes were hauling their full load for the Redhill to Reading road, and were generally being worked to their full capacity to master Dorking Bank and the slog up Pinks Hill from Guildford. Gradually the deep and wide valley began to fill up, and it became apparent that a much-needed new link between the two railways was at last being forged.

Initially there were three reception roads on the 'down' line and two on the 'up' line, with an additional siding provided on the 'up' side for berthing purposes. A new signal box was built at the southern end of the junction, known as Reading Spur box, and the whole complex was called Reading Spur Junction. It has since been corrupted to New Junction; someone probably getting an inspector's job for thinking that up! Because the bank on the GWR side was considerably higher than that on the Southern Railway side, a retaining wall had to be built on the SR side so that the whole area of the Spur could be kept on an even plane, and that wall is well worth a look to this day. Not one bucket of cement was used, as a wall of dry stone was built by two stonemasons from Gloucester. On a ride on a train from platform 4a at Reading, when the train reaches the bottom of the bank, and where the old tunnel goes under the Western Region main line on the left-hand side, the retaining wall of stone starts there, and it can be clearly seen alongside the train on the left until it graduates from a large wall to a small wall, and ends where the end of Dunkirk Siding used to be.

Within a few months of completion of the Spur, it was generally believed that an attempt was made by a German daylight raider to knock it out. I was on an engine running towards Reading Yard with a local goods working at about 3p.m. that afternoon when the German aircraft flew low over us and, at the same time, we heard the explosion of the bombs which had fallen in a stick of four close to the Old Town Hall. I'm sure it was a Wednesday, and 73 people were killed. We stood in Reading 'down' Yard and the air was full of red brick dust, which drifted and fell so that by the time we went to the depot the engine was covered in it. It was coincidence that I had to go to the Town Hall to renew my cheese ration form on that day, and as I got there, I saw about eight bodies lying in the road, and I particularly noticed one dear old lady who used to sit on the steps of the Town Hall selling papers. I was with the same driver the next day and we talked about the bombs. He pointed out to me that if the bomb-aimer had delayed by about one second, the stick of bombs would have fallen on Reading Spur. From the placing of the bombs that fell, and the direction the plane was flying, I think he was about right. We heard later that the plane had been brought down near Newbury, and that the pilot had received his training at Reading Aerodrome, Woodley, in 1934.

During 1940 and 1941, whenever term-time came to Wellington College, my girlfriend used to go home to Abertillery and whenever I could get some time off I would go to see her, changing trains at Newport and catching another train up the Western Valley line. On these trips I often went up to the engine at Reading, and asked if I could ride there. It was always a 'Castle' class locomotive, and on a couple of occasions I asked the fireman if I could have a go with the shovel — after first of all asking the driver if he minded. I took over at Swindon, on the 2.37p.m. service from Reading one Friday, and the first surprise I had was the weight of the shovel. It was much heavier than the one we used on the Southern Railway but having volunteered, I was certainly not going to complain. I had watched a good many firemen handle these engines, and I adopted similar tactics of firing quickly round the box and keeping a big fire under the door. I was generally firing up more often than the regulars, mainly because I wasn't loading the shovel so much, but I found the injectors easy to operate and usually handed over at Newport with a full boiler, and with the steam pressure gauge near the mark. My trips to Wales ended after 6th April 1942, Easter Monday, when Kathleen and I 'tied the knot'.

The GWR engines always fascinated me. To listen to a 'Castle' or a 'King' class locomotive leaving Reading with a heavy train for Paddington, the clear sharp whipcrack of the four exhaust beats was music to me. I have been in bed three miles away, on a still cold night, and have still plainly heard them. It was always my opinion, and still is that, somewhere in the design of his front ends, Churchward had mastered the secret of the perfect clearance of exhaust steam, and no other designer ever quite captured it to the same extent.

There is little doubt that every locomotive depot has its characters, and during my time on steam, Tommy Flight comes immediately to mind. Tom was made redundant at Slades Green, and moved to Reading in 1926 as a fireman. He passed as a driver during the early years of World War II, and was driving regularly from that time. He was, and still is, at 82 years of age, a very good gardener, typical of the type who could make a shilling where others might starve. I was his mate on the 1.35p.m. stopping goods from Reading to North Camp, stopping en route to shunt the yards at Crowthorne and Blackwater. My girlfriend came on to the platform to see me, and Tom talked her into riding on the footplate to Blackwater and catching a train back to Crowthorne, which she did. The engine was No. 1802, a 'River' class tender engine converted from a tank engine. There cannot be many women who can claim to have ridden on a steam engine heading a goods train.

It is worth recalling two other incidents concerning Tom Flight. Again on the 1.35 goods, while shunting at Blackwater, he spotted a goose in a wide ditch running alongside the line. Tom saw this as a useful addition to his smallholding so he borrowed a sack from the shunter, caught the goose, and tied it in the sack with its head and neck extending outside the sack. He then put the goose in the box on the Class U locomotive where the clothing was kept. On arrival at Guildford Shed Tom left the engine, going to the office for instructions, but the foreman however had noticed the engine coming to shed and had sent a pair of men to take it out on a special. Tom's fireman was up the back of the tender taking water when the other fireman climbed on to the footplate, so the first thing he did was open the box to put his bag and coat away only to be met by an angry hissing goose. We were told that he left the footplate with one jump.

Every day for many years, an engine went down into Reading Gasworks, and one of the perks of the crew was to be able to take a gallon can in and get it filled with creosote for 1s. 0d. Those that wanted any gave their can and money to whichever crew was on the duty, and received their creosote later. Tom brought two cans in, and the crew filled them with water from the tank and handed them back. The trouble was they were for Tom's neighbour, who had lived next door for thirty years with never a cross word. Two days later the neighbour poured some of the 'creosote' into an old saucepan to get on with the fence, and his next move was to bang on Tom's door asking him what game he was playing and did he take him for a fool. It was later resolved, and Tom was exonerated, but all the footplate staff at Reading were highly amused at the incident.

Together with other octogenarians, Ralph Powell and Bill Lund — both men who I have worked with on the footplate for a good many miles — Tom Flight turns up every Tuesday and Friday afternoon at the British Rail Staff Association Club at Reading to play crib and solo. Fred Wilson and a younger retired driver, Len Hopkins, were also regular attenders, besides a good many Western Region retired members who I know well enough, but only Jack Price and Alfie Eastman by name. Trips are arranged to places like Barry and Neath, to take on other railway pensioners at various card games, and Tom Flight does all the writing and arranging. Fred Jarvis, Gordon Thorpe and myself, who retired together, have also joined the clan and incidents during the days of steam are often relived.

Soon after the war, a Reading driver told me of an incident in which he was involved during 1941. It had been serious at the time, but six or seven years afterwards he realised an amusing side to it which he was prepared to relate. He was working an empty eleven coach ambulance train from Reading to Redhill, destined for Folkstone, via Ashford and, although the train was empty, it was all crewed up with medical officers and trained nursing staff — all military people. All signals at Guildford were green, giving a run right through the station and into the tunnel at the southern end of the station, but between the platforms and the tunnel the train had to pass through a 30m.p.h. crossover and, because he had not been checked at all, the driver admits striking the crossover at about 35m.p.h.

Before the train was properly under control, about four coaches had passed through the crossover too sharply. The men on the footplate were not aware of it, but several items of crockery and glass were broken during the rough ride though the crossover. On arrival at Redhill, the irate officer in charge of the train stormed up to the engine to take the driver to task. The fireman was leaning out of the cab, completely unaware of what had occurred at Guildford, and the officer said to him, 'What do you think you are, a couple of steeplechase jockeys?' Quite innocently, and without any thought of sarcasm, the fireman replied, 'No sir, but my father used to live next door to Gordon Richards'. This took the wind right out of the officer's sails so he turned on his heels, in a worse temper than ever, certain in his mind that the fireman was trying to be funny at his expense. In fact, the fireman was simply stating a fact, as his father's claim to fame was that he had lived next door to Gordon Richards, and his son never lost the opportunity of making it known.

In recalling the incident the driver was certain that had he taken an on the spot verbal dressing down, and apologised to the officer. That would have been the end of the matter, but in the event, the officer had obviously resolved to take the misdemeanour to the top, with the result that the driver concerned was banned from working any ambulance trains for the duration of the war.

Wokingham, located seven or eight miles from Reading, became a busy junction during World War II as traffic to Feltham, Brentford, Acton, Willesden and Temple Mills all went via this town. Also, the passenger service to Waterloo ran over the same old London & South Western Railway routes. Heavy freight and considerable passenger traffic also passed through Wokingham for Guildford, Redhill and the southern and south-eastern coastal areas, while heavy traffic from these areas for the Great Western Railway at Reading was often blocked back to Wokingham and Bracknell on the 'down' side. There was only one route to the GWR at Reading, the old bank, which is now the normal route for passenger trains from Waterloo to Reading, or from Gatwick and Redhill to Reading, using platforms 4A and 4B. There was one long siding on the 'down' side at Wokingham, and freight traffic from the SECR side could be signalled into the siding by a ringed arm signal on the same post as the outer home signal. The departure end of the siding was about 80 yards short of the crossing gates and the platforms. Freight traffic from the L&SWR lines could only be berthed a Wokingham by running down through the station, then setting back into the siding on the 'down' SECR line.

On the 'down' side, just beyond Wokingham Station, there was a short siding leading into the goods shed. It was decided that if a siding was made from the goods shed road, to run parallel with the 'down' line, it could be extended to the Skew Bridge which carried road traffic from Wokingham to Reading. This project would greatly increase the berthing capacity at Wokingham, and would take some of the pressure off the Southern Railway's goods yard at Reading. There was one stumbling block to the scheme; at about 40 yards beyond the point where the goods siding led back off the 'down' line, there was a solid brick bridge known as Church Road Bridge. It was built to allow normal 'up' and 'down' traffic to pass through, but any siding that ran alongside the 'down' road had to somehow pass through the solid walls of the bridge structure. It was decided that part of the bridge structure would have to be pulled down brick by brick, and a new archway would be built to allow for the extension of the siding to the Skew Bridge. To do this, a siding had to be laid from the goods shed road up to the bridge and an empty open wagon was propelled along this new siding up to the bridge where the discarded bricks would gradually fill the wagon, which could then be replaced by another empty wagon.

Dick Lester, my regular driver, and I, had a Stirling F1 class 4-4-0 on the first day that the operation commenced. We moved up to the bridge with the empty wagon, and it wasn't long before the four men working on a cradle were tossing bricks into the wagon. When the truck was sufficiently loaded, the shunter in charge asked us to pull forward. I was driving the engine and, after about 60 yards, I heard a strange noise at the front of the engine and stopped. On getting down from the footplate, and walking to the front, I could see that the leading bogie wheel was derailed. This meant that the breakdown vans had to be sent for from Reading Locomotive Department, the breakdown gang had to be called for duty and an engine and crew had to be arranged and then sent off to Wokingham to re-rail the engine. Once the breakdown gang arrived, it didn't take too long to put the engine back on the rails and, afterwards, the workers in the gang reloaded the breakdown vans with the jacks and wedges which they had used and adjourned across the road to 'The Rising Sun' for refreshments.

The Chief Permanent Way Inspector was in attendance and some one, probably the shunter, had told him that the fireman was driving the engine. This had obviously convinced him that the derailment occurred because the engine was going too fast for the shunt movement, and I heard him tell the depot foreman that he would like the engine to set back to the bridge again and then make the same forward movement, this time with the driver in charge of the engine. The foreman explained that it was his job to re-rail the engine, and that he would have nothing to do with any further movements until the track had been properly examined. In spite of this, the Permanent Way Inspector was adamant that the same move should be made, under the same conditions, and he would accept the responsibility. We then set back, on the instructions of the Inspector, and came forward again on his orders to the shunter. We moved along at about the same speed and, at the same point, the noise started and, for reasons of his own, Dick Lester didn't respond quite so quickly to the shouting as he might have done.

I climbed off the engine, and walked to where the Inspector was standing at the front of the engine. The whole bogie was now derailed, as were the leading driving wheels, meaning that six wheels were now derailed instead of two. The depot master walked away in disgust as he now had to get all the breakdown gang again, for a bigger job than ever, within five minutes of having done the job that they came to do. I stood close to the Permanent Way Inspector, and saw him push his trilby hat back on his head, then, talking more to himself than to me, he said, 'I shall have to put this down to the sinking of the virgin sub-soil'. The new siding was eventually finished, proving to be a great asset as a berthing point and, in later years, as a good shunting neck.

One night's work, during 1942, has always remained indelibly with me. I signed on at 7.30p.m. with Bill Lund, who was just about the nicest man I ever worked with. The date was 19th August, and we coupled up to a twelve coach ambulance train on Reading Spur but were not informed of our destination, although we were informed that the train was fully staffed with nurses and doctors. With Class U engine No. 1627 we made our way to Guildford and then, after a delay of about thirty minutes, moved on from there to Godalming Goods Depot which was near Farncombe, the first station on the Portsmouth line. We were under the control of the Railway Transport Officer at Guildford, who was also in liaison with the RTO at Portsmouth, both men being in close contact with military officers. At about 2.30a.m. we propelled back on to the main line, and made our way as far as Liss where we were stopped. After further delay we had to run round our train, and work back towards Guildford. Working tender first we went up through Woking, turned off the main line at Byfleet Junction, and then traversed Addlestone Junction and Virginia Water Western Curve to arrive at platform 5 Ascot. By now dawn was just breaking and after a while, in the half light, relays of small four berth army ambulances drew up alongside platform 5. Many casualties on stretchers were lined four deep all along the platform, and were steadily loaded into the train.

Just after 6a.m. we left for Reading, where a Great Western engine took over while we went to the shed. It was not until several days later that we found out that our casualties, mostly Canadians, had been involved in the daring raid on Dieppe. Years rolled by and I was always puzzled about the many and varied moves we made that night, until I picked up a library book on the Dieppe raid and in it was a chapter about an ambulance train that they had all ready, but didn't know where to send it. The raid had started at dawn, on 18th August 1942, the majority of survivors had been rescued by the Navy during the evening and were offloaded at Portsmouth and Newhaven. There were a lot that came back later who had been delayed at Dieppe, and the boat that brought them back had missed the tides and was cruising up and down waiting for instructions, while at the same time, with military information, the Railway Transport Officers were also awaiting instructions, but were trying to make calculated guesses as to where the train would be required. Eventually the troops were landed at Newhaven, after some trouble in clearing other ships from the berthing point, and the injured were then taken by road to Pinewood Canadian Hospital, a small place near Crowthorne. Here they were given emergency treatment, and were then driven the few miles to the ambulance train at Ascot Station. The war dragged on through 1943. Our daughter Wendy was born on 2nd April of that year, and I began to realise that I now had greater responsibilities.

Through 1943 and into 1944 I began to work more and more with Driver Bill Lund, who was a very good mate and always considered that the fireman was as equally important as the driver when working on the footplate. His logic was based on the fact that the driver couldn't even start to do his job until the fireman was doing his job properly, and that the ability of the fireman, his observance of signals and mastery of the skills of firing a locomotive were the primary requirements which allowed the driver to efficiently perform his duties. Bill Lund had moved to Reading as a driver from Ramsgate in 1940. He had been a fireman on South-Eastern main line trains running to and from Folkestone, Charing Cross, Dover and Victoria for seventeen years, on the Class E 'Coppertops' converted by Maunsell and finally several years on the 'Schools' class. He told me that the old experienced drivers, on the Class H tank engines, could watch the reflection of the flames on the bunker, and if the engine wasn't steaming freely by that means could tell the fireman where to fire to the engine. After the Grouping of the LSWR and the SECR several interchanges of locomotives were tried with a full load over the Charing Cross to Folkestone route; a

'Coppertop' would be so hard pressed for water that the injector would fly off at Westgate because the tender was empty.

My old mate Bill Lund told me of an incident that occurred when he was a fireman. He was the fireman on a Class E locomotive, one of the old SECR 'Coppertops', and they were about to run into Whitstable Station to stop at the end of the platform. They would have been running at about 40 to 45m.p.h., and, as they reached the approach end of the platform, a woman jumped from the platform into the path of the train. She was obviously killed, and the normal delays awaiting police, ambulance, etc. occurred before the train could continue. Bill Lund and his mate had to attend the inquest and, after medical evidence of injuries and cause of death, the first railway witness was called. This happened to be a young junior porter of about fifteen years of age, who had been on the platform when the woman jumped and was, in fact, an eyewitness to what had occurred. After explaining what he had seen he was then asked by the coroner, 'What did you do next?' Without stopping to think, and obviously intent on telling the truth, he said, 'I ran to the 'Jolly Sailor' to fetch the platelayers'.

Bill Lund told me of an occasion when, as a fireman, they were booked to relieve at Ramsgate and work to London but as soon as they saw the engine, Class T9 No. 313, his mate's heart went into his boots, as he could not see how he could be expected to run a fast train with that thing, but before many miles had passed, he was pleasantly surprised, and at Charing Cross admitted that the engine was faster and far superior to the 'Coppertops' they were used to. After a time one of the fastest timed trains over the road, 'The Granville', was regularly headed by a Class T9.

CHAPTER THREE

Dummy Tanks — Doodle-Bugs — and Accidents

There is little doubt that steam locomotives have always held some sort of fascination for most people, because wherever there is an engine working in steam today there will always be many people of all ages admiring the locomotive. When steam was the main motive power on British Railways, it was mostly the enthusiasts and spotters that were present. Providing they were well-mannered in their approach, I found it difficult to refuse to let a yougster have a ride during the fourteen years I was driving steam engines. Shunting at Earley, Wokingham, Bracknell, Ascot, Sunningdale, Crowthorne, Blackwater, North Camp or Ash, providing all shunting was within station limits — I know I have sent many a lad home happy and perhaps a bit grubby. The only thing that ever worried me was the possibility of an exploding gauge glass and the ensuing panic that might occur, leading to an accident. Even the enthusiasts have probably never experienced this, or are aware of it happening quite frequently. There are not many men, who worked on the footplate for any length of time, who didn't tend to panic the first time it happended to them.

The gauge glass is a slim glass tube, of which there are generally two on the footplate boiler front, and they simply record the level of the water in the boiler. The purpose of having two is in the event that one may blow, a train could still be worked. The gauge glass has a protector of specially toughened glass, to protect the crew from flying glass if it explodes. I was quite young when I first experienced it; there was a loud bang and in the next second the footplate was full of steam, and I was wondering what would ensue. Fortunately the driver reached into the steam and closed the top cock of the water gauge column, and when the steam cleared everything was back to normal except that we were now running with only one gauge glass. It occurred several times when I was driving, and I have closed the cock usually to see an amazed youngster when the footplate cleared of steam.

During the war every freight train was loose-coupled, which meant that the engine and the guard's brake van were the only means of bringing the train under control and stopping it. Because of this the guard was a very important person, and it was a necessity that he knew the route and gradients completely and used his brake correctly. At Reading we were fortunate as our goods guards were the very best, and could always be relied upon. As a new man joined the goods guard's link at Reading, he was taught how to work a train to Redhill or Feltham, so that right up until I finished freight work, in 1963, if you had a Reading guard behind you the job would be done correctly from the rear.

Whenever there is a short down gradient followed by a fairly sharp up gradient, with a loose-coupled freight train of any length and weight, it is inevitable that unless something is done about it, that as the second half of the train is still on the down gradient and the front part has met the up gradient, the rear half will be travelling slightly faster causing the couplings to slacken towards the middle of the train, eventually giving rise to a fairly violent snatch a little further on. The effect of this snatch was inevitably taken by one coupling which, in a good many cases, would fracture causing the train to become divided, with the accompanying dangers of a train running in two parts.

The bridge at Winnersh Halt Station and the road bridge at Little Sandhurst were two typical places where trains would break away if not handled properly, as were Ascot and Virginia Water on the 'up' Feltham road. The way to avoid the snatch was for the guard to apply his brake while the whole train was on the down gradient, thus keeping the couplings out tight. The driver worked the engine lightly, not shutting off steam, up to the bridge where he would work the engine very heavily until all the train was through the bridge. By this means there would be no snatch, because the couplings were fully extended throughout.

It can be understood that during the blackout of the war or during fog, all concerned had to know exactly where they were. During the six months prior to the Normandy landings in June 1944, many heavy ammunition trains were worked away from Ascot West by Reading men, invariably double-headed, the labels on the wagons showing 'Live Ammunition – Detonated'. Ascot West Sidings, where an Ordnance Depot had been set up, had many lengthy sidings, and with so many soldiers stationed there it had a large NAFFI and its own garrison theatre where films where shown. It was not unusual to wait from four to six hours for a train to be assembled, and I enjoyed 'bangers and mash' in the canteen a good many times before eventually leaving for Redhill.

An interesting incident which took place during the spring of 1944, was when we left Reading Shed with Class N engine No. 1816, for a special train to Redhill from Reading Spur. After leaving the engine line at Reading Junction the move to the Spur was over the 'up' line, where the points and ground signal just beyond the Kennet Bridge authorised the move back on to the train. Never knowing the type of train, we were always keen to see what sort it was as we ran past it on the 'up' road. The make-up of the train was about 36 large Churchill tanks, and Bill Lund and I were sure that although we had a Class N locomotive we must be well overloaded if we took them all. The Redhill guard gave us the load, which he said had been left for him by the GWR guard, and he commented that it was well under the load for a Class N engine which was equal to 60 vehicles. Although my driver queried it, the guard said there was nothing he could do about it. We decided that all we could do was have a go, but we expected an almighty struggle, because although we had worked tank trains before, twelve to twenty was about the most we had seen in one train.

I had the fire all ready for a heavy slog up to Earley, and when we set out my mate tried to get a good run at the bank up round Palmer Park by not pulling the engine up too much, working with the big valve of the regulator and $3\frac{1}{2}$ bars on the reverser. When we cleared the Spur, and expected to really feel the weight of the train, to our surprise, we were marching along almost like a passenger train, so that when the engine was worked much lighter in the small valve and the lever was on 2 bars, it was still doing well. We stood and looked at each other in amazement, and then looked back to see that all the train was still coming. There had to be an explanation, but we were unable to think what it could be.

We came to a stand at Guildford and I went back to the first vehicle, climbed up on to the wagon and looked at the tank. When I tapped it with a key it didn't have a metallic ring at all, so I tapped it again somewhere else and there was no doubt it was wood. I tried the second one and it was the same, so I hurried back to my mate with the news. We both thought we must be in a bad way if we were fighting this war with wooden tanks, but the real objective emerged some time later; they were decoy tanks, built and painted exactly like the real thing. These tanks, and there were a good many other train loads, were being placed in sidings and other areas within about five miles of the coast around south-east Kent. The boffins knew that German reconnaissance planes were regularly taking photographs of coastal areas, and wanted to give the impression that the build-up for an invasion force was taking place in that area; in fact, it all took place in the New Forest area of Hampshire, and Dorset.

In May 1944 I moved to the passenger link at Reading with Driver Bill Chown. He was not the best of mates, because he expected me to do all his oiling besides my own work when preparing an engine. When we finished a day's work by cleaning the fire, somekbox and ash pan of an engine, he left me to it as soon as the engine was turned, whereas almost all other drivers stopped and assisted the fireman in the disposal of the engine. Most of our work was over the Redhill road, but we did have a van train turn where we took an engine from Nine Elms Shed to Waterloo, leaving at 6.50p.m. and unloading parcels etc. at the main stations to Reading, later shunting at Twickenham and Staines.

Although I was with this driver for 4½ years I eventually adjusted to his ways enough to make things tolerable, and I learnt quite a lot from him. He was absolutely fearless on a fast train, no matter how much of a rough ride we might be having, and with a fast train to Redhill he was the only driver I knew who would open the regulator again as soon as Dorking distant was seen to be off, whereas most drivers did not apply steam again until the whole of the train had run through Dorking. During fog he had implicit faith in me seeing the signals, and seldom looked out himself, but his ability with the application of the vacuum-brake was brilliant and never failed to amaze me.

During blackout conditions stations had very little light showing, usually with just an oil lamp at the approach end of the platform with a cowl fitted to avoid any glare showing upwards. I was always sure we were going right through the stations, such was the speed at which he approached them, but without fail, when we came to a stand, the end of the tender was exactly level with the end of the platform; I resolved to take particular notice of his system of braking. To allow him to achieve such perfection in such visibility without ever putting his head outside the cab, (and there was no doubt that his speed of approach and run-in to a station was much sharper than any other driver) there had to be some system. By watching where he made his first brake application, the amount of vacuum he destroyed at that time, and making mental notes for every station, his method gradually evolved — he had a mark for every station, both 'up' and 'down'. Sometimes an overbridge, sometimes an underbridge or a platelayer's hut, a distant signal or an advance signal for the opposite running road. At these points he closed the regulator, put the reversing lever into the coasting position and then looked up at the brake gauge and applied 10in. of brake, holding it in that position until almost into the station when the brake was fully applied. The application handle was lifted almost immediately and the large brake ejector was used, so that the train did not stop with a violent jerk, but with all brakes off, ready to move again.

On one occasion, when coming down from Redhill to Reading with the 9.34p.m. train, I told him that Chilworth distant signal was at 'danger', but he didn't brake as there were crossing gates at Chilworth and the distant was rarely cleared for 'down' trains, although the home signal was invariably off. As we rounded the left-hand bend towards the station, I spotted the home signal was at 'danger' and shouted to my mate. Down went a full application of the brake and I thought, you've had it this time, we won't stop short of this red light. At about 20 yards from the signal it changed to green and my mate blew the brake off, but we came to a stand with the signal alongside the cab. When the brakes came off we pulled into the station, and after a minute or two I was looking for the green light from the guard to proceed but I couldn't see him or his lamp, although I knew he was only riding three coaches back. I told my mate, and we decided I should go back to the van and see what was wrong. One van door was open but there was no guard, which was strange because I had seen him join the train at Gomshall, the previous station. While I was standing there, wondering what had happened, I heard somebody calling, and looking towards the back of the train, the guard, Horace Barton from Reading, came staggering towards me, covered in scratches, and with a parcel under his arm. He told me that he was so used to my mate running in at speed that when we stopped outside he thought he was in the platform, so he kicked the parcel out, and stepped after it, only to fall about 4½ft. and roll down the bank through thick brambles.

Bill Chown had started as a cleaner at Exeter in 1904 on the LSWR, moving to Strawberry Hill Steam Depot as a fireman in 1910 and becoming a driver there in 1916. He used to speak about Dugald Drummond as if he knew him personally, always referring to him as 'Old Drum'! It was a practice of Drummond's to make spot checks on locomotives at Waterloo and ask to see the lamps; there had to be four, and they had to be spotlessly clean. If they didn't conform to his standards the fireman would be warned on the spot that if he was caught again with unsatisfactory lamps he would be sacked, providing he was the man who had prepared the engine. My mate had known several firemen who had been sacked by 'Old Drum' for being caught twice with dirty lamps. This attitude was prompted by the fact that there had been several serious accidents involving fast trains colliding with light engines and, at the enquiries, there was evidence that the tail lamps of the engines were badly lit and were difficult to see. There is no doubt that a properly trimmed and cleaned oil lamp gave a very good light, with its magnifying front and a reflector in the body of the lamp, but if there was any smoking of the lamp it would soon blacken the glass with soot, making it impossible to see from any distance.

One thing that this driver had done on a good many occasions, always with the Class F1 engines, was to uncouple the links on the front end, drop them over a fraction and then tighten them up again. By this means the engine gained a slightly greater opening of lead steam when in forward gear, making her better able to start a heavy train, but on the debit side, it was lost to the engine in reverse gear allowing very little ability to start a train, because of the restricted opening of the admission ports in reverse gear. It would have been considered a serious offence at that time to be found interfering with the setting of a locomotive's motion, but I believe my mate was a genuine throwback to the days when drivers regularly carried out their own fitting requirements, and were expected to do so. I think it may well have been the practice in the West of England for drivers to regularly alter the links and foregear eccentrics on the Class M7 tanks if they thought it would help, — and old habits die hard.

On one particular trip to Redhill we were given Class L11 4-4-0 No. 440 of Drummond design, these engines being known as 'Big Hoppers' by the men. It is true to say that ex-SECR men hated them, saying they shied when you put a tail lamp on them because it was too heavy to pull along. Engine No. 440 wasn't doing too well with the six coaches and two vans to Redhill, and I was struggling for steam all the way, so Bill Chown said we would 'muzzle' her at Redhill to improve her steaming ability. He obtained a piece of chain from the fitters' shop, pushed a spanner through the middle link and then laid the spanner across the blastpipe, with the chain dangling down the blastpipe. The introduction of the triple blastpipe was a more up to date method of trying to achieve the same objective, to increase the force of the blast from the exhaust steam as it left the chimney. This would create a vacuum in the smokebox and the only contact with air, which will always rush to destroy a vacuum, was from the footplate, over the fire and through the smoke tubes, thus livening up the fire on the way and improving the steaming qualities of the engine. I must admit that on No. 440 and mostly on Class M7s, when I tried it myself as a driver, it did have the desired effect!

Redhill Locomotive Depot was an uncomfortable place to be in August 1944, and I was there nearly every day. 'Doodle-bugs' were coming over at regular intervals, and although we stood and watched them, if the engine stopped on one we always crouched down tight against the tender, waiting for the explosion, with our fingers crossed. It didn't seem so bad then, because, for the first time in five years, it now appeared that we were going to be on the winning side and, generally speaking, although they did a lot of damage and killed thousands of people, we were fascinated by them. I know, in one hour, I counted 38 going over Redhill, and I can well believe that the district of Penge had more flying bombs in one square mile than any other area.

The engine tooling system had gone astray again, mainly because of the often unavoidable fact that over a period of time, firemen would lock up an engine toolbox, put the key in their pockets and go home. Men signing on would request the keys for the engine they were taking into service and they would not be available so the only alternative was to break the locks with a coal pick. In a year or so from its inception, the system of keys for engine lockers was no longer in operation, but a new idea was being tried. The fireman would collect spanners and hand brush, etc., put them in the bucket and then take the bucket and firing shovel to the stores where the engine number was chalked on them. This seemed to work at smaller depots like Reading, but to prepare an engine at Feltham or Nine Elms was always a rat race. Before you could start to prepare an engine everything had to be scrounged from other engines; oil bottles, paraffin bottle, feeder, firing shovel, bucket, spanners, hand brush and even tools from the tender, like darts, prickers and clinker shovel, had to be found. Engine lamps and gauge lamps were also required before it was possible to start preparing an engine for service. Inevitably it meant going to the foreman in charge and telling him what was still required, and the next engine into the shed would be used to supply tools for the next one going out. It was some years after the war before a sufficient stock of tools was available, and things then settled down, with all engines being properly tooled again.

I was on at 8p.m. one night when there was a telephone call from the signalman at the junction signal box, complaining that a cow in a wagon close to his box was making a terrible noise. It had been transferred from the GWR at about 8.30p.m. that evening, having been dispatched from the Totnes area in the morning. It was destined for the Haywards Heath area, and the next service from Reading was the 5.30a.m. van train to Redhill. The signalman signed on at 10p.m. and made his complaint at 2a.m., stating that it had been bellowing for four hours to his annoyance and worry. The

56

shed engineman who was in charge mentioned it to me, and I told him that I thought it wanted milking. I then got on with the job of turning an engine and then afterwards cleaned the fire, smokebox and ashpan. While I was on the tender taking water the man in charge asked if I would have a go at milking the cow, the request having come from Control at Woking, after my opinion of what was wrong had been conveyed to them.

I had never milked a cow, but I had watched it being done a good many times, so I obtained a torch and, with my driver, made my way to the signal box. We could hear the cow well before we got there and, on arrival, informed the signalman, who came down from the box to see if he could help, bringing another torch with him. After scrambling into the cattle truck, the cow willingly rose to her feet and stood quietly while I got on with the milking by torchlight, wasting the milk until the signalman decided to fetch a saucepan. After being satisfied that I had exhausted the supply, I handed the saucepan out and, between us, we closed the truck and went to the box for a cup of coffee made with fresh milk. There was no more noise from the cow, so I had obviously hit on the right solution for the poor animal, and although the scrambling in and out of the wagon had caused me to be rather smelly, I felt it was all worthwhile.

I was now nearing 25 years of age, and although I had attended the mutual improvement classes fairly regularly, I had to start thinking about taking the driving examination within the next few years. At Reading, we were very fortunate as several drivers had regularly given their own time to teach younger men a full knowledge of the rules and regulations concerning railway duties, and also a complete understanding of the workings of a locomotive; the making of plug trimmings for big ends, small ends and side rods, tail trimmings for slide bars and pistons, etc. all had to be learnt. The changing of gauge glasses and the packing of glands also had to be part of our instructions, so that we could be considered to be efficient enginemen. Without doubt the most capable lecturer at Reading was Driver W. R. Powell, who was generally known as Ralph. His main attribute was his patience with the 'not so bright', and his obvious realisation that it was not his job as a lecturer to try and show how much he knew, but to impart to his pupils, by slow easy stages, the subject under discussion, being prepared to wait for slow learners if necessary. No doubt there were many men of this type throughout the railway system, and if a debt is owed them my nomination at Reading would have to be for Ralph Powell.

The amount of traffic that had been moved over the Reading to Redhill road during the war years must have run into millions of tons, and yet in spite of the many difficulties involving long hours on duty, heavy trains that were often loose-coupled, steaming difficulties and the black-out, I can only recall two serious incidents. A Redhill driver, working a fully loaded ammunition train, some time in 1940, had a young and inexperienced sixteen year old as fireman. The train was composed of sheeted wagons, 35 vehicles which were equal to 60, which was the full load for the Class N engine provided. As the train approached Gomshall, the driver looked back along the train and saw that a vehicle about twelve back was alight; the sheet covering the wagon was in flames. He brought the train to a stand as soon as possible, and set about carrying out the rule applicable to burning vehicles in a train. This entailed uncoupling behind the burning wagon, drawing forward to a safe distance from the rear part, unhooking from the front of the burning vehicle and then pulling forward to a safe distance again, thereby isolating the burning vehicle. The driver had carried out all these moves himself, as the guard seemed not to be immediately aware of the fire or had possibly gone back to protect the train. The driver could not waste time in explaining to his young fireman what was required, and obviously felt that it was incumbent upon himself to get on with it. This meant running backwards and forwards four times, and while he was pulling forward on the last move a terrific explosion occurred. The wagon was blown to matchwood, and a pair of wheels and an axle were blown about 60 yards into a field. The rest of the train was saved, and the driver was awarded the George Medal.

The other incident occurred at Shalford Station, when a Class Q1 Austerity engine left Shalford Yard light engine for Guildford Shed. It was not crossed to the 'down' road at the first available crossover but was allowed to move on the wrong road to the next crossover, located at the Guildford side of Shalford Station, where the engine was now standing at the ground signal controlling the crossover, waiting for a change of aspect to green for the movement on to the 'down' road and on to Guildford. The Reading crew of Driver Griffin, Fireman Dowl and Guard Bill Ward, who was probably one of the most reliable and conscientious guards at Reading at the time, left Guildford for Redhill with a full load of petrol tanks, the train being hauled by one of the heavy and strong War Department good engines which had been moved into the area to tackle heavy loads, and reduce the need for double-heading. Shalford distant signal was cleared to green, this being an important signal with heavy trains as it could be seen before reaching Shalford Junction, and the driver would extend the engine to get a run at the long climb from Shalford, through Chilworth, and up Shere Heath. It was all set up for the violent collision that occurred when the train came through the bridge in Shalford Station. The impact knocked the light engine some distance, and caused a good many tanks to derail and tip over towards the rear of the train. The Reading crew were awarded the British Empire Medal because although injured, both returned to their engine and assisted in moving forward with vehicles that were not derailed. The freight guard, another Reading man, was awarded the British Empire Medal for proper attention to protection duties, although badly shaken. Because of the accident, many thousands of gallons of petrol were spilled in the marshy area around the River Wey, between Shalford Junction and Shalford Station. The signalman had been under the impression that the light engine was standing on the right road at the 'down' starting signal, but must have wrongly freed the frame in the signalbox to allow the 'up' road signals to be cleared. The crew of the light engine were also in the wrong, because although standing about for long periods awaiting signals was commonplace, it was the driver's duty to send his fireman to the signalbox, after waiting three minutes, to carry out Rule 55, the object of which was to remind the signalman of the position of train or engine. Had this been done, the accident would have been avoided.

CHAPTER FOUR

Early Driving Years

By 1947 we had two more children; Jimmy, who was born 17th March 1945 and Linda, who arrived on 3rd June 1947. Jimmy must have been born with steam and coal dust in his blood. He left school before the end of his last term, to start as a cleaner at Reading early in 1961, and was a fireman until Reading Southern Steam Depot closed in 1965, moving to Basingstoke as a fireman on steam and then, after 1967, on diesel. In 1968 he moved to Chertsey as an electric train driver and then to Strawberry Hill when Chertsey Depot closed, later moving back to Basingstoke as a mixed traction driver where he is at present.

In 1948 my regular Driver Bill Chown had a long illness and was off for about six months, so during this period I was getting different drivers every week working in place of my mate. They were often passed firemen around my own seniority and the job was usually shared, so I would often be doing 50 per cent of the driving. Eventually it was learnt that my regular mate, who was past 63 years of age, would not be taking up his position on the main line, and would be starting back on shed duties. This meant that the senior driver in the goods link would be moved up as my driver in No. 1 link. I had been aware of the possibility and I knew who it would be, none other than my old mate from early wartime days, Dick Lester. We had always got on well together, and knew each-other's ways very well. Dick would always insist on doing the firing one way, and it was a revelation to watch him perform with a shovel. Some of the much older drivers, who had been retired for some years, had told me that Dick Lester was the best fireman they had ever had, and I could well believe it.

There was a depot of electric train drivers who signed on at Reading Station, and Dick Lester was waiting for the next vacancy which might occur in the ten positions at the station. These were men who had moved from the steam depot in seniority order. A further eight positions became available at Ascot in 1939, but any driver on the Southern Railway could apply for these vacancies as Ascot was a new depot. The coverage for sickness, leave etc. had to be provided, at both depots, by Reading Locomotive Steam Depot. A special link was formed at the steam depot in 1939, known as the dual panel, which comprised eight drivers with steam rosters who would be trained to drive electric trains, thereby providing coverage for Reading Station and Ascot motormen, as they were then known. The men in this link were given rostered Sunday duties on electric services, to ensure that they were kept in touch with the stock and that they maintained the route knowledge. The problem was that although there were drivers who wanted a motorman's position, they were not prepared to be subjected to 'day-by-day' alteration to cover electric services, and preferred to wait and perform their settled steam rosters until a permanent electric position arose. This meant that instead of eight drivers in the steam dual panel, only three applied, which was certainly insufficient to provide proper coverage and, because of this, five firemen, who were passed to act as drivers, were trained to drive electric trains and became part of the dual panel. By 1949 Reading Motorman's Depot had been increased to twelve, and Ascot's to ten. Men moved from the steam depot for these positions, creating vacancies in the dual panel for three men.

As the senior fireman, I was told that I would be taking the driving examination on 3rd March 1949 along with G. Thorpe and J. Hockley, the same two men who had moved to Feltham with me ten years earlier. All three of us satisfied Inspector Arthur Langdon that we would become competent drivers, and within a few weeks, the three of us were booked to attend the training school for electric traction at Selhurst. There were twelve of us in the class, and the inspector who trained us was an ex-Brighton man named Sirrell. He was very good at his job, spending the mornings in the classroom and the afternoons out on the stock. During the afternoons he would completely disable a train by removing certain fuses, and each of us in turn had to discover the fault and make the train available for service. During the second week we were out on the track, satisfying the inspector that we could operate the brake correctly on normal service trains. Our brake testing on main line stock was done at Victoria, where we each had to drive a twelve coach Brighton express stock train into the dead end platforms. Each driver had to do this three times to the satisfaction of the inspector. Having passed the examination there followed a period of route learning and riding with drivers, who would sit you in the seat so that experience could be obtained in the practical use of the brake. It was then up to each of us to sign the necessary route card, and notify local management that we were ready to be taken on as dual drivers. I moved from the passenger link to the yard shunters, this was to ensure that I was available for driving duties at short notice, as it was possible to relieve me by upgrading a cleaner to firing duties. My driver, Dick Lester, moved to Reading as a motorman at the same time as I passed for driving.

I was performing driving duties all through 1949, either on steam or electric services, and it has always been my opinion that although we were being paid less than an appointed driver we were far more useful. One typical week's work that I recall was as follows —- Monday, Class N engine with the 7.42 Reading Spur to Redhill heavy loose-coupled freight, and return from Redhill to Reading with a relief Continental cross-country train; Tuesday, a rugby special from Reading Spur to Twickenham formed of a twelve coach train and Class U No. 1627, empties from Twickenham to Clapham Junction for cleaning, light engine to Nine Elms for turning and water etc., light to Clapham, empties to Twickenham and work the rugby special back to Reading for the Western Region. Wednesday and Thursday I was covering a Reading electric duty; the 2.28 Reading to Ascot service, the 3.16 Ascot to Guildford, the 4.15 twelve car Nelson electric main line stock from Guildford to Waterloo stopping at Woking, the 5.37 Waterloo to Ascot via Woking, Sturt Lane Junction, Frimley Junction and Camberley, the 7.26 Ascot to Waterloo and the 8.24 Waterloo to Reading. Rest day on Friday. Saturday, relieve Eastleigh men on 'King Arthur' class No. 744 *Maid of Astolat*, at Reading West Station, then work a football special of Portsmouth supporters for Nottingham, working to Banbury going to Banbury Shed to await the return special from Nottingham, then work back to Reading to be relieved by an Eastleigh crew. The work was always interesting but being a passed fireman, available for any steam or electric duty at late notice, meant that it was very difficult to make any social arrangements in advance. Although we had a rostered signing on time as firemen, it was seldom used, and we could be several hours removed from that time. Flexible rostering was commonplace to any driver that had worked through the grade of passed fireman, but on becoming an established driver, with a regular rostered duty, it was possible to look months in advance and know what duty you would be covering and what time you signed on and off.

During the summer of 1949 I was booked to conduct a Reading Western Region driver from Reading to Redhilll. The train was a relief Continental train for Margate and Dover, and started from Wolverhampton. It was an eleven coach train headed by 2-6-0 No.

6363, a class that was in regular use on passenger services on the Western Region at that time, although eleven coaches was an exceptional load for an engine of that size, bearing in mind the stiff gradients of the Redhill road. After the Wolverhampton crew had been relieved, I made myself known to the Western Region driver and his fireman while they were taking water. I was 29 years of age, but the fireman must have been well into his 30s, and was obviously several years older than me. The accepted timing past Wokingham was eleven minutes and we had taken thirteen. I knew the Western Region driver worked to Feltham, so he knew the road as far as Wokingham Junction, but at this point I had expected the driver to hand the engine over to me but the way things were, to a man of about sixty years of age, I suppose he thought I was too young. We were four minutes late at Guildford, the other two minutes being lost because the driver had shut off steam at Sandhurst when we started to get a bit of a run on; although I told him it was all right to keep steam on, he ignored me, and opened the regulator again between Blackwater and Farnborough. After leaving Guildford the engine stuck to her task, and the climb to the top of Dorking Bank was only about one minute out from the timing. We then had a long steady downhill run of five or six miles through Dorking, but soon after that the gradient was steadily uphill, through Betchworth and Reigate, dropping again into Redhill. The weight of the train soon increased the speed, and we were well over 60m.p.h. when I spotted that the Dorking distant was 'clear', and told the driver to let her run and that we had the road. This was the general practice with all Southern drivers, although my old mate Bill Chown would have applied steam once Dorking distant was 'clear'.

From Dorking distant signal the station could be seen about one mile or so away, with a straight falling gradient, and a steady left-hand curve from the start of the platform. The speed was still increasing and the Western Region driver reached for the brake, so I again told him he needn't brake, but he could see the station rapidly approaching, and could not see any track beyond the station. The next second he made almost a full brake application, and said it was too fast for the engine, so in less than a mile from Dorking we were down to about 30m.p.h. The severe brake application had resulted in all the speed being taken out of the train, with the prospect of mainly uphill work the rest of the way to Redhill. In normal circumstances the speed and momentum of the train from Dorking would have taken us through Betchworth and Reigate without really feeling the weight, with the engine being lightly worked to maintain speed. As it was, we never got above 30m.p.h. the rest of the way to Redhill. We later worked back to Reading on a stopping passenger service, the 4.04p.m. from Redhill, with six coaches and a normal run.

About a fortnight later, our depot master called me into his office and wanted my written explanation on a guard's lost time ticket for twelve minutes, which was due to the Western Region driver having written on it 'Southern pilotman in charge of engine'. I explained to the depot master that I had never been in charge of the engine, but stood behind the other driver who, at times, ignored my instructions. I wrote below his remarks 'Western Region driver refusing to work under Southern pilotman's instructions between Crowthorne and Betchworth'. I heard no more about it, but chatting to one or two Western Region men I was told that the driver concerned was known to be a bit on the nervous side where speed was concerned. I certainly didn't blame the engine, although I know I could have easily timed the train with one of our own Class U locomotives, but that would mean a fresh engine from Reading, and I would doubt such a performance, working through from Wolverhampton as No. 6363 had done.

The messroom at Waterloo was a very busy place, with perhaps 100 or more drivers from the South-Western Division taking their 'Physical Needs' breaks at different times during the day; there would sometimes be forty to fifty men there at one time. The duration of a 'PN' break averaged about forty minutes, and was rostered within a duty between the third and fifth hour. About 9a.m. was always a busy time, with men who had signed on around 5.m. to 6a.m. taking their breaks, and there were often several men at the stoves cooking themselves a breakfast of bacon and eggs.

I was covering a Reading electric duty which signed on at 5.30a.m., taking a break at Waterloo at 8.50a.m., so I went to the messroom, made myself some tea and sat down to eat my sandwiches. One man was frying bacon and had left his egg on the table, while another had put two hard-boiled eggs on the table with his sandwiches, and was making a can of tea. An accepted leg-puller, who was just leaving, switched one of the hard-boiled eggs for the egg that would have been fried. Shortly afterwards the man with the bacon fetched what he thought was his egg and was doing his best to crack it on the side of the frying pan. While this was happening, the man with the boiled eggs tapped one sharply on the table, where it splattered in front of him. There was no immediate laughter but a lot of inner amusement, but then each of the drivers concerned was prepared to blame his wife, until someone told them what had happened. They only had to say that the person had left about five minutes ago, and it was then obvious who the culprit was, as his practical jokes were well-known; I believe he paid for that prank several times afterwards.

On another occasion I was sitting next to my brother in a full room, when he nudged me and showed me a firework, it being 5th November. I put my lighted cigarette below the level of the table, touched the blue paper and then my brother threw it along the stone floor under another full table. We certainly didn't expect the ensuing panic that occurred with the explosion. One man who was leaning slightly backwards in his chair lost his balance, but as he fell he grabbed at the men each side of him and took them with him. Another man, who was doing his best to hang on to the door handle, explained afterwards that he thought the floor was splitting open because we were two storeys up. Fortunately nobody was hurt at all, but when everything settled down my brother had tears streaming down his face from laughing so much.

On 28th December 1950, our second son Adrian was born. He too started as a cleaner at Basingstoke in 1966 and is now a driver at Reading Electric Depot, having seen the end of steam traction at Basingstoke in 1967 and completing about 200 duties as a fireman on steam engines, up to July 1967.

Covering electric duties at Ascot and Reading, but signing on at the steam depot, always involved additional time in travelling and walking. Notices regarding normal speed restrictions or alterations had to be examined at the signing-on point, and late notices at the electric depot were also the responsibility of the dual drivers. the two car electric units ran coupled as four car trains or any multiple of two, up to twelve coaches. Normally, over the Reading/Waterloo/ Ascot/Guildford route, the trains were eight cars from Waterloo or Reading during the rush-hour periods, breaking down to four cars at other times.

Riding with an old Reading driver in 1949 on a two car unit, I was surprised that he was unable to stop at Frimley Station. The brake gauge showed that the air pressure had fallen to about 30lb. from 70lb., and listening for the sound of the compressors it was obvious that they were not working. The driver did not seem particularly disturbed for he had obviously experienced this before, and went straight to the three fuses controlling the operation of the compressors. After testing and finding the blown fuse the compressors started working and we were soon back in business, losing about four minutes in setting back to the platform after obtaining a full brake. Talking about it afterwards, the driver pointed out that by placing the brake gauge high on the left-hand side of the cab, with just a very dim light in the cab roof, the designers had made it very difficult for any driver to keep his attention on the brake gauge so that invariably, when the compressors stopped, failure to stop properly was the first warning. The trains would start with low air pressure and could be stopped normally with no problems if the pressure fell to about 40 to 50lb.; it was below that pressure that the inability to control the train occurred. When talking about this to other regular electric drivers, there were very few who had not experienced the problem of loss of compressors and air when working on two car units. It did not occur on four cars or over, because other compressors would maintain the air supply. In almost every case, when incidents occurred because of a gradual fall in brake pressure, it was never reported because usually the loss of time was covered, and the driver would have been in trouble for not keeping his eye on the brake gauge. It eventually happened to me a couple of times, although I discovered it in time to avoid any incident, and fell in line with the rest in keeping quiet about it.

In October 1952 I worked the 8.24p.m. Waterloo to Reading service, a four coach train. I was booked relief at Ascot, walk to the rear two coaches and detach, then work the same train to Guildford as a two car, after the front two coaches had left for Reading. Everything went as normal until the slightly falling gradient approaching Wanborough; I knew I was not going to be able to stop in the platform there. The two car unit went right through the station before coming to a stand and, looking up to the brake gauge, I was not surprised to see that only 30lb. of air was showing and that no compressors were working. I changed the defective fuse and soon obtained a full brake, set back into the station and then proceeded. Nothing was reported, as usual, with minimal delay being covered by the guard. Within a fortnight of that incident, on 8th November, Driver Harry Tullet of Aldershot — a man in his sixties who I knew very well — was unable to stop with a two car train when approaching Guildford. From the distant signal at Guildford there is a long steadily falling stretch of approximately 1½ miles, and here the trains would comfortably reach 60m.p.h. in the coasting position. A 40m.p.h. right-hand curve started at the outer home signal, and all drivers would brake there so that the train took the curve at the correct speed. Driver Tullet would have done the same thing, and it would have been at this point that he realised that he had a defective brake because of a gradual fall in air pressure. He was now approaching red signals, at a speed of about 40 to 50m.p.h., and still on a falling gradient. Driver Eddie Greaveshurd, who started cleaning at Guildford a few weeks after

66

me, was leaving Guildford Shed tender first to Woking, with 'Black Motor' 0-6-0 goods engine No. 693 running light, and as he was going through the crossover on to the 'up' road to Woking the runaway electric train came into violent collision with the engine. Driver Tullet was killed instantly, and two passengers were also killed. This tragedy caused heated discussion among the regular electric train drivers resulting in several open meetings, at which the mens' representatives were finally instructed to inform management that two car units would no longer be operated. No four car trains would be broken down into two trains until something was done about the position of the brake gauge, the basis of the argument being that it should be within the natural vision of the driver, at eye level.

Dual drivers were not directly concerned in the ultimatum to management, but obviously we were approached by the representatives of the electric drivers to stand by their decision and not operate the stock as two car trains. The matter was resolved by a simple method which obviously should have been an inbuilt feature of the units; a control governor was fittted to all units, which operated when the air pressure fell below 50lb. By this means the master controller or dead-man's handle became inoperative when the contact was broken at the governor bridge, and the train could not be moved. When air pressure was restored to above 50lb. the governor bridge reseated, making the contact to give control again. When the units had been fitted with control governors, a white spot was painted on the outside of the cabs to indicate this and, at the same time, the brake gauges were lowered to the eye level of the driver.

The early 1950s was a terrible time for the hated smogs in London, although thick fog seemed to be prevalent in all areas at that time. It was a miserable experience to go to work at about 4p.m. and crawl about all night, never daring to avert your gaze from the exact position at which the next signal was expected. In country areas, where obvious landmarks were few and far between, it was quite possible to virtually get lost and lose one's bearings for a time. Then came the dreaded fear that a red light may have been missed, and the inner feeling that it was pointless to keep going even at a crawl. I defy any electric train driver, who worked for several years through that period, to deny that he had undergone that ordeal until suddenly a signal or bridge appeared and then, when it was recognised, invariably he had not gone as far as he thought he had. On occasions there were some whose confidence went and they would go sick, while at other times, some men refused to go further without another driver in the cab.

Throughout the period of severe smog and fog I particularly remember working a fast Portsmouth to Waterloo train from Guildford, formed of twelve coaches of Nelson stock which regularly covered the route on fast trains. Stopping at Woking only, visibility was just a few yards and, on arrival at Waterloo, a dear old lady was waiting by the cab door to thank me and offer half a crown. I tried to explain that her thanks and appreciation were enough but she insisted, and said she could afford it. In 33 years as a driver this was something very rare, as passengers generally walk past the cab without realising how much a 'thank you' is appreciated by the driver.

CHAPTER FIVE

Runaway Engines —
Disasters at Barnes and Lewisham

In 1951 the promotional scheme from steam to electric was altered again, with steam drivers no longer being allowed to refuse to cover electrical duties on an 'as required' basis. The original dual panel of drivers or passed firemen was disbanded and a new system was formed, in which a link of eight drivers were given a set of duties comprising steam and electric rosters. Only men from this link could progress to motormen at the parent depot; in our case Reading. This meant that some drivers who had been waiting for an electric vacancy, were forced into the dual link to maintain their interest in a regular electric job. It must be remembered that on the Southern Region particularly, the man who had twenty or more years to go before retirement had to seriously consider moving on to electric traction, and it was strongly rumoured at that time that the Reading to Redhill line was next for electrification.

I was appointed as a driver in the dual link in 1952 along with a regular fireman, and together we had two full weeks of rostered electric work, the other six weeks all being steam duties. On the weeks when I covered my electric rosters, my fireman worked with other steam drivers. When I had a steam roster I could be altered on to an electric duty at late notice, as electric duties would always take priority because my steam duty could be covered by another driver who was not trained to cover electric duties.

My regular fireman was Stan Hutchinson, who was a young married man with two children. At that time there was plenty of opportunity for overtime and it was nearly all disposal work; engines which had been left by other crews required turning and watering while their fires, smokeboxes and ash pans required cleaning. The time allowance for each was roughly 1½ hours and as the engines were required for further duties, when we arrived in the shed the foreman would often meet us, and ask us to deal with a couple of other engines as well as our own. As we were both bringing up young families, my mate and I invariably agreed to work overtime as we both needed the money, but I always left it to my mate to decide. We were not alone of course, as most younger men with children would take the opportunity of earning a little extra. Stan Hutchinson and I got on very well together. Once I knew he was competent I regularly allowed him to do the driving, partly to give him experience but also because I liked doing the firing.

We had one duty on which we worked, the 5.40p.m. Reading to Redhill service, returning with the 8.33p.m. train to Reading. Both were passenger trains, and from Monday to Thursday we had a Class U engine while on Friday we had a Class T9, No. 708. My mate did the driving up to Redhill each day, and on the Friday everything was normal until running down Dorking Bank. It was dark at this time, and when we could see Dorking distant signal I told him to get control of the train a bit earlier as the free running Class T9, with its Stephenson's Link motion, was going a lot faster than the Class U engine would be. He started to apply the brake, but not sufficiently, and by this time we were fast approaching Dorking Station. I shouted to my mate to 'drop the handle' to fully apply the brakes, but we went right through the station. My mate was astounded, and started apologising for letting me down, but it had all happened so quickly. I then pulled the reverser back and set back into the station, the guard waving us back with a green light. Platform duties were attended to and everything was all right. The distance to the next station, Deepdene, was about one mile, and when we stopped there two passengers came up to the engine and asked if we were a ghost train, as one passenger was certain he had seen the headlamps of the engine coming from Dorking which had then disappeared. The person concerned had obviously seen us just as we were setting back into Dorking Station, and as my mate was at the platform side doing the driving I left him to do the explaining.

On a night in 1953, sometime in February, an engine moved from the back road of Reading Shed, up through the shed and along the exit road from the depot, becoming derailed at the catch points outside Reading Junction signal box. The engine, No.1615, finished almost upside-down in the dip at the bottom of the bank up to the Westen Region, very close to where the old tunnel is now. There was no one on the engine, as it had been disposed at about 9p.m. and it moved off at about 9.40p.m. The driver responsible for the disposal of the engine was charged with leaving the engine with no handbrake on, the reversing lever in full foregear and the cylinder cocks in the closed position. It is unlikely that a driver would leave an engine without making sure that the handbrake was applied and, bearing in mind that the last move of the engine by the driver would have been with the lever in reverse gear, it is hardly credible that any driver who was stabling an engine would arrive at the berthing point on to stop blocks, then wind the reversing wheel through the proper mid-gear position into full foregear. The other supposition, that the cylinder cocks were not opened, may have been correct, but it was stretching the imagination to assume that the regulator valve was blowing through to such an extent that a build-up of steam would move an engine for about 350 yards on a rising gradient. The driver was reprimanded by management at an inquiry, but they must have had some misgivings and were going through the formality of simply blaming the man because it was his responsibility, and there was no evidence that anyone else was to blame.

Within two months of that incident I was on duty at 9.30p.m. spare for one week, and on the Wednesday my fireman was E. J. Hockley who had passed for driving duties with me but was not, at that time, an appointed driver. Our first duty was to relieve a Feltham crew, who had worked a coal train from Feltham Yard to Reading, and who came to the locomotive shed at about 10p.m. Because they had to leave Reading again at 10.33p.m. with another freight train we would turn and water their engine, and generally prepare it for working away again. This allowed the Feltham crew to have a sandwich and a cup of tea before working back. After securing the Feltham engine I went to the messroom and told the driver that everything was ready for them to leave — this would have been at about 10.15p.m. — and I then walked down into the shed and, along with my mate, got on with disposing a Class U engine. At about 10.45p.m. the man in charge of the telephones who was also a storekeeper, came out to me and said that he had just had a call from the junction signal box informing him that an engine had become derailed outside the box, on the locomotive departure road. My mate and I walked to the junction and there was Class U No. 1617, almost upside-down, in the same position as No. 1615 had been. Again there had been no one on the engine. I had the same fireman the next night, Thursday, and we again relieved the same Feltham crew at 10p.m. The Feltham driver referred to the incident of the runaway engine on the previous night, and wanted to know who the young lad was who was on his engine last night. He explained that he had left the messroom within a couple of minutes of me telling him that the engine was ready to leave, and although I had secured the engine they found it with the handbrake off and the lever in foregear. The driver had thought at the time that the young lad had been my fireman, but my fireman was a man in his thirties.

Both members of the Feltham crew gave the same description of the lad, and I knew at once that they were describing the cleaner who had signed on at 2p.m. and should have been off the premises at 10p.m. The Feltham crew also agreed that if required to, they would attend an identity parade. The significant point of the incident was that engine No. 1617 was the next engine that stood open in the road at the back of the shed. By walking from the Feltham engine towards the shed, No. 1617 would have been the engine that had to be passed. Thus with the information that I had, I left a note for the depot master explaining that I would call and see him at 9a.m. with some important news regarding the derailment of No. 1617. I kept the appointment, and stated the facts to the depot master. By checking back through the cleaners' rosters, the same lad had been on duty at 2p.m. as a cleaner when No. 1615 left the depot two months earlier. In spite of this the depot master would not involve the police, but he thanked me for the information and obviously intended to inform the Motive Power Superintendent at Woking. As it was, I was not aware that any progress was made in the investigation of the runaway engines. The only significant thing that happened was that within the next four weeks, the cleaner I had suspected left the railway.

In June 1954, during a long spell of very warm weather, Driver W. R. Powell was on the station pilot shunting engine from 6p.m. until he finished at about 1.30a.m. The duties included pulling the empty stock off 'down' steam trains from Redhill, releasing the engine for shed and then setting back into the required platform to form stock for trains back to Redhill. The pilot engine was also used for transferring vans and horse-boxes etc. to and from the Southern and Western Region stations. At about 9p.m., shunting duties were finished until the arrival of the next 'down' train at 9.52p.m. The engine, ex-SECR Class E 'Coppertop' No. 1737, was secured on the blocks at the bottom of platform 1. It was roughly 20 yards to the messroom and Driver Powell and his mate went there with their cups for a cool drink of cold water, with just two vans in the siding obscuring their view of the engine. At about 9.25p.m. the shunter came into the messroom with a message from the signalman; initially, the signalman was complaining that no movement of the engine had been requested by the shunter, and that the engine had passed two signals at 'danger'.

It became obvious, with the engine crew still in the messroom, that something far more serious was taking place. At that time, in fact, No. 1737 was chugging her way through Earley Station, and was increasing speed on a falling gradient. The hazard ahead was Wokingham Junction, with the possibility of a collision with a 'down' electric train. By good fortune the 'down' electric service cleared the junction at about the same time as the engine went through Earley Station, so the signalman at Wokingham now made the decision to set the points for Crowthorne and the Redhill route. It was an up gradient which might bring the engine to a stand, but the alternative route to Bracknell meant that the engine would have to negotiate a 20m.p.h. restriction at the junction and could have become derailed. There is no doubt that the engine was left with a low fire, so that she would not blow at the safety-valves during the 45 minutes of standing in platform 1, and the boiler would also be filled, thus knocking the steam pressure gauge back to about 100lb. The climb from Reading to Earley, with the engine in full foregear, must have almost exhausted the boiler of steam and water, and the low speed of the engine passing Wokingham confirmed that she was reaching the end of her tether. No. 1737 finally came to a stand between Wokingham and Crowthorne, in the dip under the Nine Mile Ride Bridge also known as King's Bridge. Driver Powell and his mate were taken by road from Reading to the bridge, where they climbed down the railway bank and rejoined the errant runaway.

I was talking to Driver Powell recently, (he is now 83 years of age), and he confirmed that the pressure gauge was at zero and that the lead plug in the crown of the firebox had fused. Another engine was sent from Reading to propel the dead engine to Crowthorne, and it was then hauled back to Reading after crossing over to the 'down' road. I estimate that the distance travelled by No. 1737 was at least ten miles, but again there was no serious attempt to discover the lunatic responsible for setting the engine in motion. Fingerprints on the handrails, handbrake, steam reverser and regulator would surely have led to the apprehension of the culprit. I was fairly certain that I knew who it was but the name of one other ex-fireman was also being mentioned, as he had been seen in the vicinity of the station during the evening when the engine left the station. With only two suspects it would have been a simple matter for the police to have asked them to account for their movements on the evening concerned, but the outside police were never informed or involved. I again spoke to the depot master, who simply told me that it was a railway internal matter and that I should not concern myself. The passage of time allowed the whole incident to drift into history, and I would even doubt that there are any official records anywhere now, that two engines that were stabled in the locomotive depot, each travelled 300 to 400 yards to the point of derailment, and that inside one year another engine travelled at least ten miles unmanned.

I believe that No. 1737 is now preserved in York Museum, in the original South Eastern & Chatham Railway livery, as an example of the 'Coppertop' class. In my view she looks as good as any engine in the museum and in fact, if I was awarding a first prize, she would win it. My opinion is probably biased because I worked for many miles on the engine as fireman and driver, and know the secret of her solo 'gallivanting' in June 1954.

One of Reading Shed's dual link duties signed on at 4.20p.m., worked the 4.58p.m. service to Waterloo, returned to Reading with the 6.34p.m. working from Waterloo which arrived in Reading at 7.50p.m., shunted to sidings and berth, took a break, then worked the 8.58p.m. train to Waterloo, departing again at 10.54 p.m., arriving back at Reading at 12.20a.m. This type of work was rostered to us as dual men, to ensure that we kept in touch with the Westinghouse brake and maintained full route knowledge of all electrified lines. During week commencing Monday, 30th November 1955, it was my turn on the roster to cover this duty for the week. It was a period of patchy fog and on Thursday, 2nd December, when working the 8.58p.m. service from Reading, I was considerably delayed between Twickenham and Barnes by the 6.34p.m. parcel train from Reading which had, in turn, been delayed at Richmond whilst unloading luggage and parcels. As a consequence of this I arrived late at Waterloo and, after changing ends and fixing the old-fashioned stencil headcode, I left Waterloo at 11.07p.m. — thirteen minutes late. The 10.56p.m. Waterloo to Waterloo via Brentford train had left at 11.02p.m. and, of course, I should have left in front of this train. The Reading services then ran first stop Staines and always ran on the 'down' local line to Barnes, so that the stopping services could use the island platforms on the 'up' and 'down' through lines. On this particular night I was surprised to be crossed to the through line at Queen's Road signal box, because I knew that I would now be following the 10.56p.m. Hounslow loop train which stopped at all stations, but would divert at Barnes from where I would get a clear run. The 10.56p.m. was, in fact, doing very well, and only checked me at Barnes. While running between Putney and Barnes I passed a freight train on the 'down' local line and knew then why I had been crossed over. The disaster which followed, within ten minutes of my train passing Barnes, caused the loss of thirteen lives and a very serious train fire, because of the failure of the proper cutting off of power from the third rail and the fact that a great deal of the stock was made of wood.

The 11.12p.m. service from Waterloo to Windsor and Weybridge left at about the right time, running on the 'down' local line and stopping at Clapham Junction, its next stop being Richmond.

The train would normally be running through Barnes at about 50m.p.h., checking to about 40m.p.h. some 200 yards past the station. Driver Flanders of Chertsey was in charge of the 11.12p.m. train, and it was freely admitted that Barnes distant signal was in the 'clear' or off position, showing a green light, indicating that the line was clear to Mortlake, which is the next station after Barnes. The 11.12p.m. Windsor to Weybridge train came into violent collision with the brake van of the freight train, which was standing at the starting signal in Barnes 'down' local platform. The signals then were of the semaphore type, with upper or lower quadrant movement to the off position. The driver of the steam-headed freight train stopped his train at the signals showing red lights, as he required the right-hand signal of the two, which would clear him to run via Chiswick and Kew Bridge Junction, via Bollo Lane, and on up through Acton. In fact, the left-hand signal was operated to 'clear', and it was obviously at this point that the signals were being operated for the approaching 11.12p.m. ex-Waterloo train to be given a clear run. The freight driver sent his fireman to the signal box to inform the signalman that the wrong signal had been operated, and that he required the right-hand signal, but it was too late because as the fireman reached the signal box the collision occurred. Driver Flanders, who I knew very well, was killed along with the guard of the freight train and eleven passengers on the train. When the accident occurred my train would have been somewhere between Twickenham and Feltham, so I was unaware of the disaster. When I arrived at Ascot they were surprised to see me, as the only information they had received came immediately after the accident, saying that it was the last Reading train that was involved in the collision at Barnes.

The Control Office for the area was at Woking, and on a normal night they would have been in regular telephone contact with all locomotive depots. They would have been compiling a complete list from each depot of which engine was on which duty, what engines were stopped for repairs or boiler attention and any relevant information regarding duty or train alterations for the next day. On the night in question, Control rang each depot in turn with instructions not to ring Control under any circumstances, as their telephone lines would be fully occupied in dealing with the accident at Barnes. The only information given was that it was believed to be the last Waterloo to Reading train and that the driver was dead, and they were awaiting further information. It didn't take long for the information to be magnified, and with no further information by midnight, it was soon around the small depot at Reading that

Driver Rowe had been killed at Barnes. I ran into Reading at about 12.25a.m. and, after berthing the train, walked to the locomotive depot to sign off. It was still foggy as I walked up the back of the shed and, as I approached an engine on the back pit, the fitter's mate was adjusting the tender brakes. He must have looked up when I was four or five yards away and, as I spoke to him he almost collapsed, as he was sure he had watched a ghost walking out of the mist. He was in a genuinely shocked condition and had to stop work and have a cup of tea, and he explained to me that it had been on his mind and he had felt he wouldn't be seeing me again.

Fortunately, incidents such as the Barnes disaster are very rare but when they do occur, they have a sickening and chastening effect on all other drivers who worked with the man who was killed. Electric train drivers get to know each other intimately, and when such a disaster occurs the necessary trust and confidence in the signalling system is badly shaken, particularly when travelling at speed. Even men with the strongest nerve take several months to shake off the niggling thought — 'there but for the grace of God go I.' I know of two efficient drivers who cracked up and came off the main line within a few months of the incident at Barnes, and although there is no direct evidence as to the cause, I will always have my own opinion.

On 7th May 1957 I was booked with my regular fireman, Stan Hutchinson, to sign on at 4p.m. and travel as passenger to Redhill to work a troop train special to Reading (Western Region) for Wales. When signing on for duty I was informed that a Reading electric driver had gone sick and that I was required to cover the turn; a younger steam driver, A. Taplin, was to cover my steam duty.

They left Redhill with Class N engine No. 1863 hauling eleven coaches. Driver Taplin was a very competent and conscientious footplateman, who had started as a young fireman during the latter half of World War II, and he would have handled the engine in the same way that most of us would have done. After the heavy climb to Reigate there was a gentle downhill run to Betchworth, falling more sharply to just short of Deepdene where the bottom of Dorking Bank was met, with the long climb up to Welcome Bridge ahead. It would be normal to take advantage of the downhill run to obtain as much speed as possible, which would take you well into the bank before feeling the real weight of the train, and Dorking would have been passed at about 60m.p.h. At about a mile or so through Dorking there was a tremendous noise at the right-hand side of the engine, with stones and ballast flying up around the cab. Driver Taplin brought the train quickly to a stand, and received a shock on climbing down to examine the engine. The front side rod had become detached from the leading wheel, and had gouged into the lineside ballast and sleeper ends. No satisfactory explantion of the cause was ever made known.

The Class N engines, although always masters of their load, were very rough-riding at speed, and the oscillation produced had to be experienced to be believed; some, of course, were rougher than others. In some parts of the front end, mainly the pendulum arm and combination links, small securing nuts had been recently replaced by metal circlips in a groove as a securing agent. A broken circlip was later found, and Driver Taplin was informed by an inspector that this was the possible cause of the breakdown. Another engine was sent from Redhill, which went to the rear of the disabled train, and the crews changed engines with the Reading crew working back to Dorking, running round the train and working to Gomshall on the wrong road, after single line working had been set up, and then on to Reading. Since the turn of the century at least, I have not heard of any similar incident in which the motion of a steam locomotive became detached when heading a train, and I missed it because a man went sick!

During November 1957 there was some apparent danger that the oil refineries at Abadan were under threat of being sabotaged or attacked, and because of this it was decided to make ready a force of special troops to be airlifted to the area. Thus on Thursday, 28th November a special troop train ran from Okehampton to Aldershot, from there they would fly from Blackbushe Aerodrome as required. The train was running via Salisbury, Basingstoke and Reading, and I was instructed to walk to Reading (West) Station and conduct the Salisbury driver to Aldershot and back light to Reading (West). The train was formed of twelve coaches headed by a 'Battle of Britain' class Bulleid Pacific, No. 34066 *Spitfire*. My experience on these engines was very limited, but the Salisbury driver immediately handed her over to me. By the time I had worked round the junction, through Reading (General) Station and over Reading Spur, I felt quite comfortable with the engine, having adjusted to the pull out regulator and the steam reverser. After clearing Earley, I was impressed by the acceleration of the engine and the steady ride as speed increased. What also surprised me was the quietness, because compared with our U and N classes the engine seemed to be whispering along. With 'clear' signals at Wokingham we were really buzzing, and the climb up through Crowthorne was not felt at all. The Salisbury driver was an elderly man of around sixty, and approaching Blackwater at speed he said to me 'You are probably going faster than you think, old chap'.

The guard of the train was Tommy Staines, a Reading guard who was an old friend of mine, and as we were both natives of Crowthorne we knew each other very well. We had to run light from Aldershot to Reading, so Tommy asked if he could ride back with us to avoid waiting for train connections. We readily agreed, and during the trip he explained that on the run from Reading we had passed Wokingham and cleared North Camp in nine minutes, according to his watch, and he was certain that it was the sharpest run he had ever made over that section. He made a point of seeing me a few days later, and stated that he had been in touch with the two signalmen at Wokingham and North Camp; both had confirmed that their logs showed that the train had cleared the two signal boxes in nine minutes. With evidence from a permanent way trackman and the service book, the distance from box to box was agreed as 10 miles 75 chains. I don't know exactly what that is in miles per hour but I would think it must have been somewhere around 73 to 75m.p.h., which was well above the line speed; at that time 70m.p.h. I then realised that it was the smooth ride and the noiselessness of the locomotive that had fooled me to some extent, and that the Salisbury driver was right — I certainly had been going faster than I thought. Had I been asked to estimate my top speed between the two points where the speed seemed greatest, namely Crowthorne to Farnborough North, I would have said it was a little above 60m.p.h.

Six days later on Wednesday, 4th December, the same engine was heading the ill-fated 4.56p.m. Cannon Street to Ramsgate service when it collided with the rear of the 5.18p.m. working from Charing Cross to Hayes, a ten coach electric train. No. 34066 *Spitfire* had been to shops at Eastleigh just a couple of months earlier, and had only clocked 3,444 miles of running since that time. Any Southern Region driver with any steam experience will confirm, that whenever a steam engine came out of Eastleigh after a complete repair and overhaul it was near perfection, and would far outshine other engines of its own class in performance, smooth riding and every other feature. This difference would be maintained for about 50,000 to 75,000 miles of running.

Driver Trew of Ramsgate Depot was the man in charge of No. 34066 when working the 4.56p.m. train from Cannon Street. He was 62 years of age, and had been a driver for eighteen years. He was described by his supervisors at Ramsgate Motive Power Depot as a loyal and conscientious worker, not so quick-witted as some, but reliable and sober. This description would probably suit many thousands of other train drivers, but then everyone has certain inbuilt characteristics which go to make up the individual; some are placid and easy going, some are slightly inhibited and natural worriers, some lack confidence while others may be slightly overconfident. The different types are obviously found in all walks of life, and it follows that a fair cross-section of all types will become train drivers. Many characteristics are obviously inherited, but it is my opinion that few other occupations will determine the attitudes of individuals to their responsibilities as that of two men working together on main line steam locomotives.

A fireman's attitude to the position of becoming a driver and performing the duties with full responsibility will, to a great extent, be determined by the behaviour of the driver with whom he worked for the greatest period of time. Some drivers would lack absolute confidence in themselves and their mates; this would generally show itself with a tendency to fidget, and interfere with the fireman's duties on occasions. If the boiler water level dropped to half a glass, or the steam pressure gauge dropped back 10lb. some drivers became unsettled, while others would remain unruffled if the water level showed about an inch in the bottom of the glass, with a loss of 30 to 40lb. of steam. Like the rest of us, Driver Trew was the product of what many years on the footplate had made him He was, without doubt, as good as any man, but I believe he was the victim of a culmination of several important factors which led to one grave error.

On 4th December 1957 he had booked on at 12.30p.m., and worked up from Rasmgate to London. With his fireman he travelled to Cannon Street to await the arrival of the 4.56p.m., arriving in good time in case the train was ready for a right time start, but in the event they had to wait on platform 6 for over an hour in freezing fog. Driver Trew had complained of feeling cold, and this would not be conducive to comfortable and alert footplate working. The 4.56p.m. service arrived at 5.55p.m. and, on boarding the footplate, Driver Trew was informed by the other driver that the tender must be getting low with water. This now, without any doubt, became his problem. No doubt the driver he relieved had previously notified the authorities of the fact that the tender was low with water, and tentative arrangements had been made for a special stop for water at Sevenoaks, to which Driver Trew agreed. Half a tank of water was the assumed amount, but with years of working on locomotives, 1ft. from the bottom can look like half a tank of water, particularly with a light being shone into the tender during darkness, and all footplatemen had been taught never to rely on tender water gauges. Did Driver Trew start to have misgivings about his water after leaving Cannon Street? Was it worrying him? One thing is certain, given normal circumstances any driver would be reluctant to knock the speed out of an eleven coach train, with the long steady climb ahead after passing New Cross Station, if it was on his mind that he was low with water.

All the evidence from drivers who worked trains over the same lines, immediately prior to the 4.56p.m., agreed that visibility was reasonable as far as New Cross; this would involve passing through London Bridge, North Kent East Junction and New Cross. After passing New Cross all drivers agreed that the fog became intense, with visibility down to 5 yards and never more than 10 yards. Driver Trew passed New Cross on a green light, unaware of the sudden change in conditions ahead of him. The line from New Cross runs through a fairly deep cutting, which continues with some retaining walls and a short tunnel and several overbridges for the ¾ mile to St. John's Station, and throughout this distance the dense fog persisted.

With the lack of usual and familiar landmarks it is quite easy to lose one's bearings in severe fog, and it is much more likely to happen if the concentration is interfered with by some nagging, niggling doubt that will not leave your thoughts. Let us be perfectly clear about the water situation. Many quicker thinking drivers would have insisted on taking water before leaving Cannon Street, it being entirely the train driver's prerogative to decide, and once he has made that decision all responsibility rests with him. All other railwaymen involved in the arrangements to leave short of water would have been blameless, and had Driver Trew insisted on taking water before leaving, the worst they could have said of him would have been that he was 'not very co-operative'. No doubt he was concerned for the travelling public — the commuters who had also been standing round in the freezing weather for a considerable time.

The green signal at New Cross would have indicated to Driver Trew that he was clear to St. John's Station. In all the years he had been driving the fast trains to Ramsgate, he had never yet been stopped at St. John's. There would have been two intervening signals between the New Cross signal, automatic No. A42 at the country end of New Cross Station, and St. John's inner home signal No. L18, L18 being the signal which was passed at danger. The signal directly following No. A42, at a distance of 440 yards, was No. L16 and would have been showing a double yellow aspect. No. L16 was St. John's outer home signal. The next signal, No. L17, was St. John's intermediate home and would have been showing a single yellow aspect. No. L17 was 423 yards on from No. L16. No.

L18, St. John's inner home, was sited at the end of St. John's Station, and was 469 yards ahead of No. L17. These signals are sited on the right-hand side of the track, but because the track from New Cross to St. John's is on a left-hand curve of 73 chains radius, driving an engine from the left-hand side, as Driver Trew was with No. 34066 would, in reasonable visibility, have allowed him to see the signals comfortably.

Trew's mate, Fireman Hoare, was an experienced man. After seeing signal No. A42 at green he started firing to the engine — it was a heavy train, and the road ahead required the engine to be up to the mark. He had generally attended to his fire at this point, and he was still firing to the engine when Driver Trew asked him to look out for the next signal. The signal in question was No. L18, showing a red light, and 138 yards beyond that was the rear of the ten coach Hayes train which was standing at a red light on signal No. M8, Parks Bridge Junction home signal. I have always been convinced that, to some extent, engine No. 34066 was so sharp that in the fog she ran through the ¾ mile from New Cross to St. John's at a much greater speed than Driver Trew had anticipated or expected. When he asked his mate to look out for the next signal he was expecting him to see signal No. L17, not signal No. L18. Any driver, and many people with an interest in railways, will readily agree and understand that from the green aspect at No. A42 New Cross the important signal for Trew to see was No. L17. He would know this signal was at least 'clear' at one yellow and it would be the important signal, giving him the information of signal aspects ahead. I am of the opinion that when his mate shouted 'red light' Driver Trew was momentarily disorientated, as No. L17 should at least have been one yellow. His lack of immediate response in failing to fully apply the brakes at that point indicate that he was probably about 440 yards ahead of where he thought he was, although it is likely that the lights of St. John's Station made him aware of his whereabouts. The visibility in the station was 10 to 15 yards, and the extent of the damage and the braking capacity of the train, led Brigadier Langley to the conclusion that the brakes were not fully applied until after the engine had passed No. L18 at red. Because of the force of the collision, the rear of the tender and the front of the leading coach were crushed together and thrown to the left by the sudden stoppage, striking and dislodging a steel middle column supporting two of the four heavy girders of a bridge which carried the Nunhead to Lewisham double line over the four main line tracks. Severe damage was caused to the first three coaches by the girders of the bridge subsiding immediately on to the train. Two minutes later a loaded eight coach train from Holborn Viaduct to Dartford was moving slowly on to the bridge, with Driver/Motorman D. S. Corke in charge. Fortunately he noticed the girders at an angle and immediately stopped his train, otherwise at least the first two coaches of this train would have toppled on to the wreckage below — the leading coach was, in fact, starting to tilt.

It is ironic that, but for a mistake by the signalman at Parks Bridge Junction, the accident would probably not have occurred, but it must be stressed that this in no way lays any blame on the signalman. The red light at signal No. L18 in St. John's Station was there to be stopped at, and the responsibility for that has always been the driver's and rightly so.

The normal right time sequence of the two trains directly ahead of the 4.56p.m. Ramsgate working would have been the 5.18p.m. Charing Cross to Hayes service, followed by the 5.25p.m. diesel-electric from Charing Cross to Hastings, but because of delays brought about by the fog the Hastings train had left Charing Cross at 5.45p.m., followed by the Hayes electric train which left at 5.48p.m. The two trains were in reverse order.

Each signal box had train describing instruments, one for receiving and one for transmitting. The receiving instrument would obtain the description of the next train from the box in the rear, and then the signalman would operate the transmitting instrument to describe the train to the box in advance. One description only is displayed at a time, and each transmitting instrument is connected electrically to corresponding receiving instruments at the next signal box. If a signalman described a train as travelling on the 'down' through route, the receiving instrument at the box ahead would follow in step and there would be an audible click as the instrument received that information. By this means each signalman would know the route for the next train in advance of its arrival, and could set up the required route.

There seems no doubt at all that the signalman at St. John's had properly described the Hastings train to Parks Bridge Junction, as the booking boy at St. John's had recorded this in the log. This would mean that the receiving instrument at Parks Bridge Junction would rotate and carry the information to the signalman there but, unfortunately, this description was not seen by the signalman at Parks Bridge Junction. As the two trains were following closely the transmitting instrument at St. John's was used again to describe the Hayes train, thus erasing the information of the Hastings train from Parks Bridge Junction's receiving instrument, which would now be describing the Hayes train.

The position then was the Hastings train standing at signal No.

M10, Parks Bridge Junction starting signal, with the Hayes train standing at No. M8, Parks Bridge Junction home signal. A red signal at No. L18 St. John's was protecting the Hayes train so there was, in fact, no need for the Hastings train to be stopped, as the route ahead was clear for it to proceed. Had the signalman seen the description it obviously would have proceeded, and this would have meant that the Hayes train could have moved from signal No. M8 to signal No. M10. Had this happened, there would have been no disaster. The signalman at Parks Bridge Junction was always under the impression that the two trains were in their correct order, and that he was holding the Hayes train at No. M10 and was waiting for a clearance to divert it to the Mid-Kent line. Even after the accident had occurred, he had reported that the Ramsgate train had collided with the rear of the Hastings train.

What was the aftermath of this tragedy? In my opinion, it was another tragedy of perhaps a lesser degree. Letters in the press, and pressure from certain commuters' associations insisted on Driver Trew being charged with manslaughter. What punishment did they want to exact from him? I have no doubt whatsoever that he would gladly have surrendered his life to be freed of the misery and mental torment that he was living through. He must have been a broken man from 6.20p.m. on Wednesday, 4th December, at the moment of the collision, and from the realisation that he was responsible for the loss of ninety lives. The right example was set by Lieutenant Colonel Wilson and Brigadier Langley, the inquiring officers, who both showed sympathy, compassion and understanding when questioning him. His evidence was described as confused and muddled, and it was probably because he was in such deep and profound shock that he could never recall exactly what happened between New Cross and St. John's stations. Driver Trew was charged with manslaughter on 21st April 1958. The jury disagreed and, at the second trial on 8th May, he was acquitted.

I have no desire to make a controversial statement, but I feel entitled to make a statement of fact. When ASLEF introduced 'work to rule' as industrial action some years later, most drivers were prompted into action by the memory of the prosecuting counsel holding aloft the Railways Board Rulebook in an attempt to obtain the conviction of Driver Trew. With due deference and respect to those who lost relatives and friends in the St. John's disaster, any campaigning that took place immediately afterwards should have been for the early installation of the Automatic Warning System (AWS) in the driving cabs of all trains and locomotives on British Rail.

I have always felt deeply sorry for Driver Trew. The long wait in the bitter cold, the possible delayed worry of how much water he had, the sudden change of weather conditions, the deceptive speed of the locomotive, the loss of familiar landmarks and the mistake of the signalman at Parks Bridge Junction, were all circumstances that culminated in that short run from New Cross to St. John's, and made drivers realise that given parallel conditions there are very few of us who would not, at some time in our careers, have agreed that once again 'there but for the Grace of God go I'.

CHAPTER SIX

Lost Time Ticket —
The 4.00a.m. Local Freight —
'Stealing' a GWR Engine

Early in 1959 a new freight train was diagrammed to Reading on Sundays. It was timed to leave Reading Spur at 9.33p.m. and was always a heavy train loaded to the extent of the engine, normally Class N locomotive. After about six weeks the train became the talking point of the depot because usually, about a week after working the train, the driver concerned would be called into the office by the depot master and handed a lost time ticket for varying loss of time between Shalford Junction and Redhill. During this period the greatest loss attributed to the driver was 38 minutes, and the least was 27 minutes. Each driver concerned answered the loss time ticket with what was generally accepted as the best answer to any loss of time with a freight train — 'engine slipping, sand working'. Each driver concerned heard no more about the matter but were surprised at the amount of time they were accused of losing, and said as much in the messroom.

Towards the end of March I was booked to work the terrible 9.33p.m. service. I signed on with Fireman B. Ward, who was also passed to work as a driver, and we were given Class U No. 1631. On the way from the depot to Reading Spur we talked about the lost time tickets, which had been issued over the running of the train, and resolved between us that 'come hell or high water' we were not going to get one. The guard gave us the load as 38 equal to 52, which was the full load for the engine, and reminded us that we were booked for a five minute stop a Guildford to change guards. I had checked the running time to Guildford, and when I looked at my watch on stopping there, we were seven minutes early. We were held to our booked departure time and, on receiving the tip from the new guard and exchanging hand signals after moving, I got the nod from my mate that both he and the engine were ready, and that I should do my best. As soon as Shalford distant was seen to be 'clear', I set about it. I freely admit that I worked the engine much harder than I would normally have done but we both felt that we were facing a personal challenge, one that we were prepared to take up providing the engine stuck it. The heavy haul up through Chilworth took some of the run out of us, but I could tell we were still running a bit sharper than we would normally have been. By the time we had reached Brook Crossing, towards the top of Shere Heath, I was beginning to feel a little bit ashamed of the way I was working the engine but No. 1631 seemed to be thriving on the hammering she was getting; her safety-valves were lifting every few minutes, and my mate's experience was keeping her up to the mark. Reaching the long downhill run to Dorking, I just used the tender brake to sit back into the train with the engine, and as it was a fine night I knew I would get an early sighting of Dorking distant signal. As soon as I spotted that the signal was 'clear' the handbrake was released, a little at a time until it was fully off, to allow the weight of the engine to gradually extend the couplings. With intermittent applications of steam, between Dorking and Deepdene, the engine was again pulling the train and we were still moving at about 60m.p.h.

On stopping at Redhill we had been 49 minutes from Guildford. I was well satisfied, as I knew that the average freight running time from Guildford to Redhill was about 1 hour 15 minutes. My mate and I went light engine to Redhill Shed quite pleased with our performance, and certain that we had cracked it. There would be no lost time ticket for us. To my surprise and disgust I was called into the office about ten days later and handed a lost time ticket for twelve minutes. I could have answered it with no trouble 'engine slipping, sand working' but I had no intention of doing that; something was obviously wrong, and I intended to try to find out what was happening. In the space for explanation of lost time I wrote 'If this train has to run any faster, it will not be running with safety', and after a chat with the depot master, he agreed to send it to the Motive Power Superintendent. In less than a week I signed on one day at about 1p.m., to be met by a Motive Power Inspector from Nine Elms. No doubt he was under instructions to give me a carpeting for having the audacity to suggest a lack of safety in the timing of the train, but he got off on the wrong foot.

After stating that people above him would not tolerate the type of reply I had given, he then asked me if I knew the road properly. My hackles rose and I walked away from him before I said something that I might regret, but after he talked to the depot master he came out into the shed and explained that he was prompted to ask that question first and, after talking to the depot master, realised that it could have been offensive. I then explained to him about all the previous lost time tickets and also that the normal running time, from Guildford to Redhill, was about 1 hour 15 minutes, and that we had done it in 49 minutes. He then began to see that there may be some justification for my attitude, particularly when I explained to him that the only way I could see someone like him was to answer the lost time ticket as I did.

By good fortune Passed Fireman B. Ward, who had been my fireman on the 9.33p.m. freight, came walking past us in the shed. I called him back, introduced him to the inspector and then asked the inspector if he would please ask him a few questions about our trip on that Sunday night. He soon learnt that B. Ward was equally as adamant as myself that the matter should be further investigated. The inspector then left the depot, after assuring me that he would trace the weight of the train and, if possible, interview the guard who had issued the ticket referring to loss of time. Within a fortnight the same inspector came back to Reading to see me, and the first information he gave me was that each vehicle on the train had been traced and the calculated load was 38 equal to 59, seven overload. The guard who took over at Guildford was an old Redhill man who, since the inception of the 9.33 ex-Reading service, had agreed to do that particular duty every Sunday night. He was using the Central Section time book, in which the departure time from Guildford was the same, but in the Central book it was designated as a vacuum-fitted van or parcel train which was timed to run from Guildford to Redhill in 37 minutes.

Either the guard concerned was having a mischievous dig at drivers, by the issuing of lost time tickets, or he was having a similar go at administration who would be responsible for the conflicting information in the Western and Central Section time books. The inspector and myself parted with an amicable relationship; he thanked me for drawing attention to the problem of the 9.33 freight while I in turn thanked him for the digging he had done, and also for giving me the full information, which was unusual.

Although the usual excuse for loss of time with a freight train was 'engine slipping, sand working' it was not generally the truth, as invariably, the real reason was a plain straightforward 'rough trip' or a shortage of steam. Drivers had learned, over many years, that to answer a lost time ticket truthfully could lead to months of correspondence, in an attempt to find out the cause of the shortage of steam. Was the fireman competent? Had the engine been correctly prepared? Was the grate area ballasted during preparation? Had the tube plate been examined? Had the smokebox door been tightened before leaving the depot? What was the standard of the coal? Whatever the reason nobody lost time on purpose, and everybody was bound to experience a 'rough trip' now and again, either as a fireman or a driver. After a 'rough trip' you were generally a wiser footplateman because something had been learned, but to have answered a lost time ticket with 'engine slipping' was insufficient and only led to further correspondence; Were the sand boxes working properly? Had the sanding gear been properly tested before leaving the depot? Were the sand-boxes properly filled? etc. From early days we were taught never to operate the sanding gear while an engine was slipping, as serious damage to side rods etc. could result. If an engine started to slip it was usually when starting or when under heavy working on a bad rail, and to deal with this the regulator had to be closed, the wheels had to stop spinning, the sanding gear could then be operated and steam applied. Answering loss of time, drivers had learned that 'engine slipping, sand working' would confound the experts in the office chairs.

One of the duties which stayed in Reading dual link for over ten years was the 4a.m. local freight from Reading Yard, Pugs Hole, to Ascot and Sunningdale. Probably no other link wanted it, because of the signing on time of 2.45a.m., and the amount of work that was involved before getting back to Reading at 10.30a.m. Arriving at Wokingham at about 4.17a.m., usually with a dozen or so vehicles, we shunted there until about 4.50a.m., then stopped at Binfield Brickworks, if required, to place coal in position and knock out any empty wagons. We then went on to Bracknell, the next station after Wokingham, to set down or pick up early morning staff, and then to Ascot to prepare and work a coal train to Sunningdale Gasworks. Again there was an 'if required' stop between Ascot and Sunningdale, at Drake & Mount's coal sidings, to place coal and pick up empties. At Sunningdale we had to run round the train, which had a brake van at each end, then work up the bank on the 'down' road to shunt out empties, and place coal at Ascot Gasworks. We were at Ascot by at least 6.40a.m., so as to clear the road for the first 'down' train from Waterloo to Reading, we swung round on the turntable and shunted at Ascot until 8a.m. We then ran light to Bracknell, shunting there until 9.10a.m., and then ran light to Wokingham and shunted there until 10.20.m., eventually running light to Reading Shed. On several occasions over the years I have woken up at about 3.15 or 3.30a.m. instead of 2a.m., dressed hurriedly, pulled on my boots although not bothering to lace them, pedalled like a maniac for about three miles, thrown my bike in the cycle shed and scrambled on the engine, sometimes in the shed, sometimes in the yard, hoping that my mate had made a can of tea.

(Above): Maunsell Class W 2-6-4 No. 31923 waits to be broken up at Feltham in 1965.

(Below): Drummond 'Bulldog' No. 30434 at an unidentified station.

(Above): Class U 2-6-0 No. 31627 leaving Guildford for Redhill on 1st January 1965. The driver is Tom Flight and his fireman is C. Jennings.

(Below): On the turntable at Ascot in 1964 is Maunsell 2-6-4T No. 31912.

(Above): Class T9 No. 120, with Driver Jim Robinson in the cab, is seen at Ascot in 1965.

(Below): Bulleid 'West Country' Pacific No. 34026 *Yes Tor* pictured on the coal road at Guildford in 1964.

(Above): 'Battle of Britain' class No. 34085 *501 Squadron* with the 2.30p.m. Waterloo to Weymouth express, leaves Brockenhurst on 26th June 1965.

(Below): On Saturday, 16th July 1960, the 8.25a.m. Weymouth to Waterloo service passes Eastleigh, hauled by 'Merchant Navy' class No. 35027 *Port Line*.

(Above): One of the last 'Merchant Navy' class locomotives, No. 35023 *Holland-Afrika Line*, pictured with the final 8.30a.m. Waterloo to Weymouth service on 8th July 1967.

(Below): With the 1.30p.m. Waterloo to Bournemouth service, 'Merchant Navy' class No. 35012 *United States Lines* rests at Basingstoke on 24th June 1966.

(Above): A photograph taken by the fireman from an unofficial position while climbing Dorking bank.

(Below): Nos. 31867 and 31868 await scrapping at Redhill Shed in 1964.

(Above): New Milton in Hampshire provides the background for 'West Country' class No. 34012 *Lapford* as it hauls a passenger train bound for Waterloo.

(Below): Sir Winston Churchill's funeral train, hauled by 'Battle of Britain' class No. 34051 *Winston Churchill*, as it passes through Reading.

(Above): A picture of myself ready to leave with my last train away from Reading.

(Below): This recent photograph shows seven retired Reading drivers with accumulative service of 343 years, (312 years spent on steam engines). From left to right;—Tom Flight (82 years old), myself (64), L. Hopkins (68), Dick Lester (85), Fred Wilson (83), Bill Lund (84) and W. R. Powell (84).

When shunting was required at Binfield Brickworks the shunter at Wokingham travelled with the guard, and it was the duty of one of them to notify the driver that a stop at Binfield was required, otherwise the train ran straight from Wokingham to Bracknell. I was well past the brickworks one morning, on the uphill gradient close to Bracknell distant signal, with about ten trucks of coal and a couple of empties, when the train seemed to be getting heavier and heavier. Looking back along the train I could see the reason; the guard was waving a red light, and had screwed the handbrake hard on. Obviously we should have stopped at the brickworks, which was now about 400 yards in the rear. It was a bitterly cold morning, with everything covered in ice during a really cold spell, and after we had stopped, the guard started waving me to set back to Binfield. I had a Class N engine, and I had wound the reverser into reverse gear and was just pegging the steam brake off and opening the regulator when I suddenly realised exactly where we were; we must be standing on or near a pair of catch points. The sleeper ends were covered in ice, and I was slipping and sliding while moving towards the rear of the train. As I neared the brake van I shouted to the guard about the catch points and, as I shone the lamp behind the van, there they were, about 5 yards away, set to run us straight off the road. The guard and shunter wanted to hold the catch points over and then set back but I would have nothing to do with that on such a risky foothold, and we took the train on to Bracknell. At the catch points there was a bank which sloped downwards to a wire fence and, on the other side of the fence, was a deep pond. There is no doubt that had I decided to set back I would have kept steam on for about 200 yards at least, and with the storm sheet up to help keep out the cold it would not have been possible to see directly to the rear of the train. With the ground frozen solid for several weeks I am sure that the brake van and its occupants would have been submerged under the pond, together with the coal, and possibly even the engine. One of my near misses!

On the lighter side, although the 4a.m. freight working was a busy duty and, at 2a.m., a terrible time to scramble out of bed in the mornings, it allowed me a few unusual glimpses of nature. In the summer, when day was breaking at around 4.30 to 5a.m., I have seen many foxes between Wokingham and Sunningdale. At Binfield Brickworks, on the opposite side of the track, there was a field bordered by a copse. On a few occasions, when shunting there, I have watched a fox jumping in the air and rolling on its back with its legs in the air, gradually moving nearer to the edge of the copse. All along the edge of the copse, rabbits were feeding, apparently mesmerised by the antics of the fox who was steadily moving nearer to that day's meal. When the fox got to about 25 yards from his chosen victim he would suddenly sprint and pounce, before any of the rabbits had a chance to move.

At about 4.10a.m. one morning, while running towards Wokingham, I looked up in the sky and saw some unusual lights, or rays of light. They were like searchlights but, instead of shining upwards, they were shining downwards through very high cloud. On stopping at Wokingham I drew the guard's attention to the lights in the sky; he was puzzled, and agreed that he had seen nothing like it before. The next day in the papers was an article stating that people in the South of England who looked up at the sky between 4 and 4.40a.m. yesterday, would have had a rare view of the Aurora Borealis or Northern Lights. It was a rare phenomena for them to be seen this far south in the Northern Hemisphere.

All locomotives carried one or two flare lamps which were used for examining the engine, particularly underneath when standing over a pit. They were like small light metal tea pots, with a woollen skein which went into the well of the lamp, and had a wick protruding out of the spout. Filled with paraffin, and with a light to the wick, they served their purpose. Along with many other men with children, as Christmas approached each year, I arranged to obtain one of the small fir trees, which grew in abundance on the railway banks in many areas, as they were ideal as Christmas trees.

The area around Ascot West was one place where a good choice was available, and the 4a.m. Ascot duty was the best turn on which to get one. The special unofficial stop for Christmas trees had to be arranged beforehand, with the connivance of the guard, who usually wanted a tree himself anyway. When there was no stop at Binfield Brickworks we could get a few minutes in hand away from Bracknell, stop at Ascot West for our trees, and still arrive punctually at Ascot. The trees we required were always picked out during daylight, when we were running light from Ascot to Bracknell, so that I knew exactly where to stop on the 'up' road during the darkness of the early morning. I had to stop just through the road bridge at Ascot West, where we were in a cutting with the bank sloping upwards away from us. The slopes of the bank were covered with well-established fir trees of about 20ft. in height, but at the top of the bank on the level grew the 3 to 5ft. trees that we wanted. After stopping one morning I lit the flare lamp and commecnced the scramble up the bank. Unbeknown to me at the time, I was not holding the flare lamp upright and paraffin was running from the well of the lamp, through the spout and the burning wick and dropping to the ground in flames. When I reached the top of the bank it was burning fiercely behind me. 'Operation Christmas Tree' had to be aborted, and we now had to become fire-fighters. Having got the fire under control, with buckets of water from the injector feed pipe, we had taken up our allocated time and had to be off to Ascot; no Christmas trees that morning.

Before leaving the 4a.m. freight working from Reading to Ascot there is one more incident I must relate — amusing to me now, when looking back many years later, but quite serious at the time. The placing of coal at Ascot Gasworks had to work with precision, as time allowed was limited and all concerned had to get it right. With a brake van each end we left Sunningdale, after running round the train, usually with sixteen to twenty trucks of coal. Stopping on the 'down' road short of the gasworks we drew forward with the coal, leaving the rear brake van on the main line. The gate to the gasworks was opened by their employees, the points being operated from the ground frame to set back on to the empty wagons in the gasworks. The coal and empties were then drawn forward clear of the points on the main line, the points were operated and the empty wagons were detached and knocked back on to the brake van standing on the main line, where the guard took charge of them. Because of the sharp curvature of the gasworks sidings no engine was allowed to pass the entrance gate, so the coal had to be detached and knocked back into the sidings where the gasworks' employees had stopped it to suit. The gate was then closed and the ground frame locked, with the engine and brake van backing on to the empties, coupling up, and working away to Ascot.

On the day of the incident, everything went right. From about 500 yards distant I saw Ascot home signal was off, and when I looked again a few seconds later it was in the on position, showing a red light. I stopped the train at the signal and, as it was just daylight, looked back towards the gasworks where the shunter was running towards us waving a red light. He was exhausted when he reached us, and explained that we had left the rear brake van on the main line because the guard had forgotten to couple it to the empty wagons. Looking to the rear I could just see the lights of the brake van, about ¾ of a mile away. There was no time for indecision, although it looked as if we were all in trouble anyway. I reversed the engine and started setting back; at the same time, the first 'up' train was travelling on the 'up' road, and we were both moving in the same direction. I knew then that the first 'down' train was only about six minutes away, but the van was soon coupled to the empties and we set off for the second time, getting inside at

Ascot to clear for the 'down' train by about two mintues. After securing the train in the yard we all adjourned to the signal box, Ascot 'A', for a conference on what had occurred. The shunter had noticed that the rear van wasn't coming so he rang the signal box, causing the reversal and replacement of the home signal by the signalman, thus alerting me that something was wrong. The signalman said it was not his intention to log anything because, as far as he was concerned, any time taken was due to shunting in section, as booked. There just remained the distance of the wrong road movement as a problem. I knew that several railway officials used to travel on the first 'up' train, and if any of them had noticed the distance between the rear wagon of the train and the isolated rear brake van there could still be trouble.

To appear to digress slightly, I think I should explain that before the panel type signal boxes came in to being, any movements in the wrong direction on the main lines were under strict control, and could only be authorised by special written orders from the people concerned in the wrong road movement. With the old signalling system of block boxes controlling separate sections, only movements performed under 'station or signal box limits' could be made in any direction without a 'wrong line' order. The guard's pink order could be issued by the guard to the signalman in advance, if an engine was unable to take the whole of a train through a section because of gradient or excessive load. The train could be divided, and the engine would take the front part forward to the next signal box, the driver carrying the guard's pink order to allow the signalman to return the engine on the wrong road for the rear portion of the train. With the driver's green order it could be issued to the signalman in advance, in the event of the breakdown of an engine, by the driver of the disabled engine. The fireman took the order forward, and it instructed the signalman to allow an assisting engine or breakdown vans to travel on the 'wrong line' to the disabled engine. The guard's white order was issued to the driver in the event of an accidental division of the train, such as a fractured coupling. Providing the two portions could be re-coupled, and no signal boxes or points were concerned in the movement, the white order instructed the driver to travel in the wrong direction back to the rear portion, re-couple, and proceed. The signalman's yellow order was issued to a driver, and authorised him to travel in the wrong direction with engine or train to the signal box that issued the order. There could be many reasons why this type of movement might be required. There were a lot of complicated procedures and rules applicable to the issuing of all 'wrong line' orders, but the

100

description I have given is sufficient to understand the position we were in with regard to the 'wrong line' movement at Ascot.

To return to the incident at Ascot, I asked the guard to make out his white order C, which would cover the movement in the wrong direction in the event that some railway official on the 'up' train may have reported something. It was not my intention to send the order in to management as I should normally have done, as we didn't want any trouble. Of course, the order should have been issued before the movement was made, but it was timed to protect us if necessary. There would have been a serious delay if correct procedure had been followed but as it was there was no delay, and the four practical men concerned knew exactly what was happening throughout. We heard no more about the incident, so I returned the 'wrong line' order to the guard after about three weeks and he destroyed it,

The medical and eyesight test for footplate grades has always been very strict, and rightly so. In 1937 a method of detecting colour vision defects was introduced into the eyesight test; apparetly it was invented by a Japanese Admiral named Ishihara, and has always been known as the Ishihara Book. Each page of the book contains a number of one or two digits worked in coloured dots, with the whole page covered in coloured dots. If colour vision is normal the numbers are not difficult to see, but if the person taking the test is unable to read the number correctly it does show a defect on a particular colour, which will be known by the medical officer conducting the test. To my knowledge there is at least one page with no numbers at all. It was agreed with the trade unions that the book could be used for the test, but that a man could not be failed on the Ishihara Book, only on the coloured lights or lanterns. Once a defect was made known the person concerned would often fail on the lanterns, because the medical officer would have some idea of the sequence in which the lights should be shown.

Driver Jack Croucher of Reading had started as a cleaner at Dover in 1916, and moved later to Ramsgate. He was a top link fireman throughout the 1920s and into the 1930s, and had moved to Reading around 1940 at the same time as Bill Lund. They had been pals together as cleaners, and their careers ran parallel through the years. When Jack Croucher fired to Driver Cotton of Ramsgate their regular engine was No. 912 *Downside*, and during that period the engine was used in a special test with large boiler tubes, an experiment that was apparently unsuccessful.

When Driver Croucher took his medical test at sixty years of age, he was judged to have failed the colour vision test, which meant removal from the position of main line driver to yard shunting duties or shed engineman's duties. Before the position is finalised the man failing a colour vision test is always allowed a retest, with a trade union representative or a friend of his choice in attendance. As we had always got on well together, and because I had taken the test a few months previously, Jack Croucher asked me if I would attend with him at his retest.

When taking the retest there were three doctors in attendance, and the lanterns or coloured lights were in the end of a dark passage which would be normal procedure at the time. The driver was seated looking directly at the coloured lights, and the doctor in charge offered me the right to stand anywhere that I preferred; I chose to stand directly behind the driver. The test commenced, and Driver Croucher was calling out the lights as the sequence changed - — red, green, red, red, yellow, green, red, yellow, green, red and many more changes of this nature. I felt confident that although the man was under extreme pressure, with his job at stake, there was nothing wrong with his colour vision. The test went on with intermixed reds, greens and yellows and then changes to a continuous sequence of greens, the light going out each time and returning again to green. After about ten to fourteen changes, with the continuous green going out and then on again, the smaller pale green fog light came up. Driver Croucher hesitated and then, after a pause, said yellow. The pale green fog light is used to assimilate the type of light that a green signal will show when viewed through mist or fog. To be perfectly honest, although I thought at the time that the last light we saw was the fog green, Driver Croucher's calling of all the lights up to that time had been so impressive that when he said yellow, I wondered if I had been wrong in thinking it was green. The lights came on in the room and the doctor asked me if I was satisfied, so I explained that there were two things I would like to say. I then said 'I feel we should have agreed beforehand on exactly what we should call the yellow light; you will be aware that the driver has sometimes called it amber, sometimes orange, and sometimes yellow. There can be no discrepancy with the other lights but we should have agreed on one name for what we are calling the yellow light.' One of the doctors said 'I fully agree with you, the man is under some pressure and we should have decided on what we would call this light beforehand so that the reading of it would be consistent.' After a short chat everyone agreed that the test would be retaken, calling the light yellow throughout.

Before the test was retaken the doctor in charge said to me 'What else was it you wanted to say?' So I then said 'Well, Sir, as the test is to be retaken, I feel that perhaps I shouldn't say what I was going to.' He said 'Please, speak up, we would rather you say what you wanted to say now.' I then explained to the doctors, within the hearing of Driver Croucher, that there was only this one mistake after a long run of green lights. In train driving conditions this would mean that a man would run in reasonable visibility for several miles seeing normal green lights, and that when he ran into a patch of fog or mist he would probably read a green signal as yellow, which was an error on the side of safety. This, of course, was tantamount to telling the driver just what error he was making and where it was being made, and was the obvious reason why I was reluctant to mention it. The doctor then explained that a colour defect is a colour defect, and there can be no latitude if a defect is found.

The test then commenced again and the same procedure was adopted, with the driver calling the yellow light yellow throughout. Eventually the long sequence of greens came up, then the fog green; Driver Croucher hesitated again, finally saying 'yellow'. I must say that the doctors concerned were more than fair. They had no desire to fail a man, but they had to do their job to a strict standard when the safety of the travelling public was involved. Throughout my 45½ years in the footplate line of promotion, I always found the medical officers to be both doctors and friends. After his failure to pass the test, Jack Croucher told me that the Ishihara Book had shown his defect in 1937 so he had always had a very stiff test on the lights, but it had taken 23 years to find the sequence that would show the defect. With only five years to go to retirement, he settled down in a shed engineman's position.

One of the Sunday duties in the dual link was a light engine trip to Moreton Yard, on the Western Region, to bring two freight trains up to Reading, one for Reading (West) Yard and the other for the Southern Region Yard. We signed on at 2a.m., prepared our engine, and left the shed at 3a.m. We had to run to Didcot, and then turn the engine by way of the triangle formed by Didcot East Main, Foxhall Junction and Didcot North signal boxes. It didn't seem a complicated manoeuvre, but many times I have been well over an hour travelling from Didcot East box and back again. Moreton Yard was about two miles from Didcot East, coming back towards Reading. I had gone to bed on Saturday evening at 6.30p.m. so that I could get up at 1a.m. Sunday for the 2a.m. duty, but on arrival at the signing-on point at 2a.m. I was met by my mate with instructions that we were to sign on, sign off and go home. My mate had come into work from Bracknell, on the last train at 12.20a.m., and there was no service to get him home until 8a.m. The shed engineman on duty and myself were not the best of friends, having recently fallen out over something else, but I attempted to go into the office to talk to him, because although my mate had arrived early and had been given instructions, I still felt that it was the driver who should be given the instructions when signing on. The office door was locked, but I still tried to get an explanation as to why we had to go home. Apart from the fact that there was no way that I could have gone back to bed after sleeping all the evening, there would have been wasted sandwiches, and also my fireman was stranded for the night. There would also have been the loss of six hours pay; we would have been paid for eight instead of fourteen hours; a fair arrangement had we been notified beforehand but unfair in the circumstances at the time. Shouting through the office door, the only explanation I could get was that it was not possible to get an engine out of the shed and on to the Western Region, but apart from that, any further questions were ignored. I then walked with my mate up the engine line to the junction signal box, where the signalman was stretched out on cushions. His explanation was that the lineman was working on the points from the Southern Region 'up' road to the Western Region old bank, and that the points would be disconnected. I then left the signal box and walked about 100 yards to where the lineman was working. I knew him well, and told him what the signalman had said. He was quite upset, and said it was nonsense, there was nothing stopping an engine coming out of the shed and running on to the Western Region. He was working on the electric cable and he had simply told the signalman that he would be cutting off the 'juice', meaning the current to the third rail. I went back to the signal box, but the signlman insisted that the arrangements had been made with the agreement of Woking Control and it was too late now anyway. We then walked back down to the shed and up into Western Region East Main signal box, where I asked them to find out if the train and guard were at Moreton Yard. The message came back that the train and guard were there, and that the Western Region were trying to cover.

I decided to walk to the Western Region Shed, where I told the foreman who we were and asked if he could supply an engine. We couldn't have been more welcome, as he had been given the job to cover but he was short of men and couldn't see how he could do it. We had now solved his problems. I don't recall the number of the engine he gave me, but I know it was a 'Hall' class named *Elton Hall*. After familiarising ourselves with the working of the brakes and injectors of the engine we set off on the locomotive departure road, towards the signal controlled by West Junction signal box, where it was necessary to telephone the signalman and inform him of our destination. On telling the signalman that we were light to Didcot for the 5.15a.m. freight train from Moreton Yard, he explained that he had been informed that the train was cancelled because no engine was available. I told him we were a Southern crew with a Western engine, and he said he would have to check with Western Region Control and would I hang on. After a couple of minutes he asked me to call back in five minute's time, as Western Region Control were going to check with Southern Region Control. After what seemed a very long five minutes I again went to the telephone and reported. The signalman said 'Just going to pull off mate, they're going to run you' and as I climbed back on to the engine the signal cleared and away we went, on the 'down' main, all the way to Didcot. We had left the locomotive depot at 4.05a.m., and we were on the train in Moreton Yard at 5a.m.

Talking to the guard, with whom I was already acquainted, he was obviously surprised to see me on the 'Hall' class so I explained what had occurred earlier in the morning, and why I had this particular engine. The guard drew my attention to the fact that the first six vehicles on the engine were all labelled as 'Green Arrow' traffic, which conveyed to all concerned at that time that this traffic was to be given priority. Because of the circumstances I decided to take the numbers of the six vehicles, the destination, and also the consignee of each one. We left Moreton Yard with 78 vehicles, equal to 100, with 38 destined for Reading West Yard and 40, including the 'Green Arrow' traffic, for the Southern Region Yard at Reading. After waiting our turn at West Yard the rear train was detached, leaving a brake van behind the 40 wagons to be taken forward to Reading Yard. We were released from Reading Yard to the Southern Shed at 9.15a.m., and the man in charge, who came on at 7a.m., asked me if I would take the engine back to the Western Shed as he had no other men available. My mate and I agreed to do this after we had had a cup of tea. It was a nice change to have worked on the Western engine, although the class was essentially a passenger engine, but I was left with the impression that the simple and efficient automatic warning system in the cab was a credit to the region, and should have been adopted long ago by all railway regions. As I went into the Western locomotive office the foreman was in touch by telephone with Paddington, checking on the engines, and he was just mentioning that the one we had taken out was not yet back. As it was, I was in time to inform him that the engine was now back, and in good order.

When I went to work on Monday at 2p.m. I learnt that the shed engineman on Sunday morning was under the impression that we had gone home as instructed, and that he intended to cause trouble because I had not obeyed his orders. In fact, he got in touch with the man who had been on Southern Control that night, expecting him to make a joint complaint regarding what had taken place. The problem was that the controller had sanctioned what had occurred with Western Control, and was under the impression at the time that it was a brilliant piece of organisation by the Southern shed enginemen. I decided to go in and see the depot master about the matter, and was soon assured by him that he was on my side and that it was his impression that, at the time, I was the only person concerned who wanted to run trains. I informed him that the 'Green Arrow' traffic would arrive at Bracknell at 5a.m. that morning, and that had the train been cancelled it could not have reached there until Thursday. I heard no more about the matter.

CHAPTER SEVEN

The Speed of Bullied's Pacifics —
Star Lane Crossing Incident

By 1962 I was aware that my time on steam engines had a limited period to run. With retirements and the concession of increased leave causing vacancies, it was obvious that within a year or so I would have to move to the electric depot at Reading, which was at the old Southern station. As I had been trained on all types of electric stock, as each was introduced into service, I would simply get short notice of moving from one signing on point to another. A medical failure of another motorman at Reading could perhaps mean driving steam on a Saturday and then moving on to electric traction on the Monday, never to work on a steam engine again. Being able to recognise this allowed me to become aware of my established affection for steam engines. Each trip, in which the performance of the engine was something of merit, became an event to enjoy.

Weekend excursion traffic from Reading to several Sussex coast resorts was very popular at this time, and as there were not many drivers at Reading who signed for the route via Peasmarsh Junction, over the single line to Christ's Hospital and Horsham, I did a lot of work over this road on the Class Q1s — known to most as 'Charlies' — a Horsham crew would then work the trains on to Brighton, Bognor or Littlehampton as required. It was a great shame that the Peasmarsh to Christ's Hospital line was closed in 1965, as not only was it very useful, but in the spring and summer it was the prettiest line I had ever seen with bluebells, cowslips and hazel trees close to the railway for many miles. It also gave the residents of Bramley and Cranleigh a very good service into Guildford for London.

It was mostly on trains over this single line that I was able to appreciate what powerful engines the Q1s were, as with ten or eleven coaches they were always the master when their steam pressure was over the 200lb. mark. With a tendency to roll rather badly during a spell of sharp running, they were far superior to the Class 700 'Black Motor' locomotives that were used on earlier excursion traffic. The Class Q1s were introduced to us at the end of 1942 as wartime Austerity engines and were built to last ten years for freight working, but they were still in operation doing useful work, to my knowledge, in 1967. Perhaps they were not everyone's idea of what a steam locomotive should look like; in fact, they were often described as ugly, but as practical engines for the work they were designed to do, I found them to be very efficient.

The awareness of leaving steam locomotives kept raising the same old niggling concern in my mind that Bulleid's 'Merchant Navy' class had never had the opportunity to prove, in special trial conditions, what amazingly fast engines they were. Given the same conditions that the Class A4s had, the record for steam locomotion of 126 m.p.h. would have been surpassed by the 'Merchant Navy' class.

In historical terms, the effective period of steam locomotives from 1830 to 1970 is of comparatively short duration, around 140 years perhaps. I count myself fortunate to have been around during that time, and to have had the pleasure of working on all types of engines as a fireman and driver, but while records will inform future generations that 126m.p.h. was the maximum attainable speed, I will always maintain that this is not necessarily true. In any other form of machinery, from cycles through motor cycles, cars, boats and aircraft, speed capabilities have improved as more knowledge became available, and I see no reason why this same maxim should not be applied to steam locomotives. There was at least ten years' additional knowledge between the design and building of the Class A4s and the 'Merchant Navy' class. The Class A4s were designed by Sir Nigel Gresley while the 'Merchant Navy' class was designed by O.V.S. Bulleid, he having been the assistant to Sir Nigel Gresley since 1923. He was, from 1930, mainly responsible for the improvements in the front ends of LNER engines. He came to the Southern Railway in 1937, with all the knowledge of the make-up of the Class A4s, and as he was essentially an inventor, he must have had his own ideas on exactly what was required to increase the speed capabilities of any new Pacific class three cylinder engine. I would not sing the praises of any other feature of locomotive design, as far as the 'Merchant Navy' class were concerned. I am aware that they have had their fair share of 'knockers', but solely on the basis of maximum attainable top speed, I remain convinced that 140m.p.h. would have been well within the bounds of possibility. Many men that I have talked to, whose opinions I respect, are similarly convinced by performances during ordinary service running, but it will be understood that in some cases men do not wish to be named when admitting to speeds in excess of

100m.p.h. A look through the book by D. W. Winkworth called *Bulleid's Pacifics* will show the number of times that he clocked ordinary trains, regardless of who the driver was, and also the times when 100m.p.h. was exceeded.

Ken Norris is an inspector at the Motive Power Training School, Waterloo. He is certainly not a man given to overstatement, and among his contemporaries his opinions are respected. He recalls one particular trip on Sunday, July 29th 1956, on the 9a.m. Waterloo to Exeter service; a train which only ran during the summer timetable. Driver Walter Bird and Fireman Ken Norris took over at Yeovil Junction and at Fenny Bridges, between Honiton and Sidmouth Junction, the recorded speed was 103m.p.h. As in all other cases of similar speeds, the engine was still increasing speed and running freely. Men who I have talked to, who have been in charge of these engines at speeds in excess of 100m.p.h., have all made the same significant point, that on each occasion the engine was still accelerating, and they had reached the point when they had to shut off steam because of line speeds. In the case of Ken Norris the engine was No. 35005 *Canadian Pacific*, but all of the class had achieved similar speeds, up to the point of having to be held back.

Driver Cyril Wilson of Basingstoke was a main line fireman at Bournemouth during the 1950s. He states that it was quite usual to be running at speeds in excess of 100m.p.h., and that even the 'West Country' class would easily achieve it. On the 2.30p.m. Waterloo to Bournemouth service, with unconverted 'West Country' class No. 34103 *Calstock*, they were recorded passing Winchester Junction well in excess of 100m.p.h. Driver Chapman was working the engine in 15 per cent cut-off and the first regulator. In 1958, with 'Merchant Navy' class No. 35008 *Orient Line*, Driver Albert Gould and Cyril Wilson, with the 2.40p.m. eleven coach Bournemouth to Waterloo service, were recorded doing over 100m.p.h. through Hook. The engine was still increasing speed, but Driver Gould had to shut off steam because he had previously been booked for speeds above 100m.p.h. with 'Merchant Navy' class No. 35023 *Holland-Afrika Line*. With the 'Bournemouth Belle', Driver Sid Peckham, with engine No. 35022 *Holland-America Line* and thirteen coaches equal to 522 tons, achieved 100m.p.h. at Winchester Junction. Signalman Ted Shelbourne, on duty at Winchfield box in 1954, timed a test train of twelve coaches to be travelling well in excess of 100m.p.h., the engine being No. 35005 *Canadian Pacific*.

There are so many instances of the maximum line speed being attained, and appreciating that there is considerable difference between 105 and 126m.p.h. I will always believe that given the

109

ideal test conditions, over the measured area between Grantham and Peterborough, 126m.p.h. would not have been in the record books as the greatest possible speed attained by a steam locomotive. The conviction of the practical men concerned, the weight of the trains and the fact that, in every case, the engines were still increasing speed, but had to be curtailed, will always hold many of us to the belief that faster engines than the Class A4 Pacifics existed.

My vacancy at Reading Station, as regular electric train driver, came up in 1963. There was a few weeks' notice but I was now aware of the obvious, and the time seemed to go very quickly. I worked a full steam duty on each day during the last week and at the end of each day, after leaving the engine in the depot, I couldn't resist looking back after walking a few yards, with a feeling that I was leaving a friend.

The winter of 1963 was very hard, and at times we were in serious trouble with ice on the conductor rail and heavy snowfalls, which tended to cause impacted snow to cut off the ability to draw current from the third rail. To be fair to the old 'BILL' stock, which was in regular service on the Reading and Portsmouth lines from Waterloo at that time, they were tough and durable and, providing you had more than just a two car formation, handled most inclement weather conditions far better than the stock that is operating at the present time.

In 1964 I had the misfortune to be involved in a serious incident at Star Lane Crossing, Wokingham, which eventually ended in the Assize Court of Reading. The cause of the trouble was the introduction of one of the first sets of automatic half-barrier level crossings, in place of the normal type of level crossing gates, which were generally operated by a crossing-keeper from a special gate box. It was Saturday, 11th July 1964, and I was working the 2.28p.m. service fom Reading to Waterloo. A protest meeting had been arranged and a crowd, estimated at 250 to 300 people, had gathered at the crossing; it seemed likely that some members of the local council were responsible for the organisation of the protest, and had also arranged for a BBC reporter to be in attendance. The declared intention of the protesters was to stand in the path of the train to see if it could stop, and although the crossing had started to operate automatically on Monday, 6th July there had been no trouble throughout the first week. The regular crossing-keeper was left in attendance to watch the operation of the barrier, and to inform the public who may have wanted information on the working of the crossing. From the driver's point of view, we were instructed to sound the whistle continuously from a point which was ¼ mile

110

distant from the crossing. The whistle on the 'Bill' stock was operated by air pressure and was situated on the left-hand side of the cab, just above the driver's brake handle, and was sounded by pushing a brass button inwards and holding it there. The crossing was positioned just after a left-hand curve, which straightened out at about 75 yards from the crossing. From the driver's seat I could only see the 'down' road crossing gates, with several people standing around, but this was not unusual as technicians had been in attendance all the week and always moved to the safety of the 'down' road when an 'up' train was due (or to the 'up' side if a 'down' train was due).

Approaching the crossing at about 55m.p.h., as the 'up' line came fully into view, I was aware that there were three people in a dangerous position on the 'up' line, directly in the path of the train. One removed himself to safety when I was about 60 yards away; I learnt later that this was the crossing-keeper, Reginald Burton, who I knew very well, and he had been remonstrating with the other two men until he could see the train coming. By this time I had stopped sounding the whistle and had made a full emergency brake application, although I knew then that it was impossible to stop short of the two men, who had now raised their arms above their heads. I have always reckoned that they were very fortunate in one respect because purely by chance, the four car train I was driving was was composed of units Nos. 2002 and 2007. This was the old Metro-Vickers stock, and there is no doubt that the Westinghouse brake on those units was much sharper than on the stock which was most prevalent over the Reading to Waterloo line at the time. With the dryness of the rails that prevailed on that day, the rate of deceleration was such that the train came to a stand with the middle of the four car train right on the crossing. When I was about 30 yards from the crossing the elder of the two men stepped to safety, but the younger man stayed there with his fists clenched and arms stretched forward towards the train. Somehow he seemed to duck under the buffer at the last split second, when I was certain that I was going to kill him. After stopping I went back to the crossing; I was shaking and obviously in a state of shock, and only recall asking the man who risked his life if he was in his right mind or was he insane, but I remember little else of the incident.

There was a delay of about 25 minutes before I carried on to London, and although I finished my duty for the day by about 10p.m., that night I started a bout of hiccups which persisted all through the night, even when I slept, and was still with me all through Sunday and when I slept again on Sunday night. It was still persisting on Monday, 13th July so I had to visit the doctor, who listened to what had happened — between the hiccups — and understood that the area of my abdomen and chest was now aching severely. A tablet cleared it up in about two hours, but all the remedies like breathing in a paper bag, or drinking a glass of water slowly, had made no difference all over the weekend.

At the magistrate's hearing, the two men were charged with 'endangering the safety of persons on the railway and obstructing a train'. One was acquitted, but the younger one, who had been the last to move, was committed to the Berkshire Quarter Sessions, where he faced the same charge on 4th January 1965. A plea of guilty, with the mitigating circumstances of 'youthful exuberance' was accepted, and a fine of about £70 saw the end of the case. I was not surprised at this, because after the magistrate's hearing at Bracknell, one of the railway detectives dealing with the case said to me, 'The big fish has got away'.

After a couple of years away from steam engines I began to see what was missing, and also the great difference between the two jobs. There were so many complicated possibilities involved in the breakdown or failure of an electric train, and they could occur right out of the blue when everything seemed to be going fine. It may not be generally known that many men just could not adapt to the operation of the straight Westinghouse brake, after almost a lifetime on the vacuum-brake, and I have always held the opinion that the transition from steam to all new forms of traction was a far greater achievement by all concerned than was ever acknowledged, and was never properly recognised.

There were far more tensions and pressures in driving electric trains. The job was generally far more exacting and onerous and, in my reckoning, I could fill two pages with the names of men who have been removed from the driver's position with heart trouble, mostly angina, blood pressure or nerves, and there are many more who died suddenly in their forties and fifties. From 1937 to 1963 I cannot recall one steam driver who came off the footplate with heart trouble or nerves, and it was puzzling that there were so many medical failures when the two jobs were compared. While it is true that between 1925 and 1939 most men were firing up to the age of forty before becoming drivers, most of these men would have started on the railways between 1912 and 1920 while the men before them, who had started between 1890 and 1910 were, in the main, driving at 21 years of age. I fired to many of the latter group at Reading and, in talking to them, discovered that almost all of them had started driving in their early twenties.

The complete failure of a steam engine was very rare; I only experienced it once, the cause being a burst tube. There were many 'rough trips', when a steam engine might come to a stand because of a combination of shortage of steam and water in the boiler, but the cause of the trouble was generally known by the two men on the footplate, and between them they would usually get moving again. Without doubt, a couple of 'rough trips' did a lot to cement the relationship between driver and fireman, and the experience was always invaluable to any fireman who hoped to become a steam engine driver. Although it was unavoidable, single manning brought loneliness and the loss of a second pair of eyes, but if there is one factor that marks the difference between the two jobs it was, in my opinion, 'job satisfaction'. It is difficult to analyse or attempt to discover the reason for the many medical failures, but the opinion held by many is that a young driver of 21 years of age has taken so much tension and pressure at 45 or 50 years of age that a fair percentage will succumb medically after 25 to 30 years of driving. Against this theory is the fact that many steam drivers of 45 to 50 years ago were driving trains for well over forty years although the difference, of course, is the form of traction on which they performed their duties. It is certainly true that train speeds are generally faster — 70m.p.h. is commonplace on local and semi-fast services — but, of course, the braking systems have improved to give correct control at the higher speeds.

I do not consider myself any sort of expert, but I have worked many years with the steam men (between 1937 and 1962) and also many years with the single-manned electric train drivers (from 1949 and 1982). Job satisfction was the difference between the two jobs, coupled perhaps with the loss of respect from the travelling public, who would invariably acknowledge the crew of a steam engine but would walk past the driving cab of an electric train as if there was no driver required. Perhaps this is inevitable, but I will always hold the opinion that of the two distinct jobs, steam train driving was less exacting, and certainly far more satisfying.

Working regularly on electric trains had its advantages; the job was much cleaner, there was no more tender first running on bitterly cold days and nights, no more visits to the eye department of the hospital because of coal dust or smokebox ash causing painful injury to the eyes, and no more scrambling out of bed at times like 2a.m. to start work, or getting home at 3 or 4a.m. after signing on at about 7p.m. We were fortunate at Reading, as our earliest signing on time at the electric depot was 5.15a.m. and our last train back at night arrived at Reading at 12.20a.m., providing things were running normally. Of course, it was not the same at all electric depots because at places like Waterloo, Wimbledon Park and many other berthing points, men would be booking on and off at all times throughout the day and night.

Over a period of many years I had learnt to respect the obvious dangers of the electrified line, or the third rail as it is commonly called among railwaymen. As a young man, some time during 1940, I had the terrible experience of seeing two Canadian soldiers almost burnt to cinders in the carriage sidings at Guildford. Apparently they had come through heavy rain to the station, but had missed the last train to Aldershot. It had to be conjecture about what really happened afterwards, but it seemed that they saw a train in the sidings and decided to get into it and sleep until morning. The first one to attempt the climb up to the train must have stood on the third rail and reached up to the handrail at which point, with wet clothing and hobnail boots, he would have taken the full force of the electric current. It also appeared that the other soldier may have tried to assist the first one, and suffered the same fate.

In spite of knowing the dangers of the third rail, most of us as firemen had a touch of it at sometime or another. Perhaps the most likely way was when deciding to get a bucket of water to have a wash. The injector water feed from the tender was usually opened, and when the water ran out of the injector waste water pipe the bucket was filled. If the electric rail was that side there was always some current running back up the water, and when the bucket was held there you could feel a twitching in your arms as you took a mild electric shock.

Struggling to push sixteen trucks of coke out of Reading Gasworks on one occasion, my mate decided to get a fire-iron from along the tank and dart the fire up. As he pulled the dart through the observation window and allowed it to swing out over the side, it touched the electric rail just momentarily, but for a few seconds it was hanging suspended from the palm of his hand, although he was trying to let go of it. Eventually it fell, but it left a nasty burn in the palm of his hand.

Perhaps one of the most sensible things that management have arranged over recent years, is to pick certain drivers with experience, who are capable of talking to children, to explain to them the dangers of playing or venturing anywhere near the railways, with particular emphasis on the dangers of the electric rail. The driver makes contact with all the schools in a given area, seeking the permission of the headmaster to arrange a visit to the school. The driver is always very flexible, and will visit the school several times if necessary. This is to cover the several age groups, and although the talk given to twelve to sixteen year olds is obviously different to that given to 5 to 8 year olds, the same message is driven home to receptive minds, and it has proved very effective. It is to the credit of headmasters and teachers that they have fully co-operated in this very sensible exercise. I have had the unpleasant experience of seeing a young lad killed on the electric rail. It is a most disturbing and upsetting time for all drivers when it occurs, and all children should be warned by their parents not to play anywhere near the railways.

CHAPTER EIGHT

Bill Simmonds —
Sir Winston Churchill's Funeral Train

Early in 1965, the Reading Southern Region steam depot was closed, with most of the men moving to the Reading Western Depot and becoming Western Region employees. My son Jim, who was a fireman, decided to stay on the Southern Region and moved to Basingstoke, along with two other firemen who took the same option. At the same time the Southern guards and drivers who were at Reading (South) Station were also moved to the Western Region, with the guards becoming Western Region employees and being fitted into links or rosters with a Southern link included. The sixteen Southern electric drivers remained Southern Region employees for all purposes, and were in the unique position of being employees of one region stationed within the boundaries of another region. Many of the Southern freight guards, who had often covered electric trains with us, had opted for the Western Region freight link, and we rarely saw them again after the move had taken place. We worked with several new men from the Western Region, as their guards had the option to work in the new Southern link, covering the electric duties and also the workings over the Guildford – Redhill – Tonbridge line.

One of the characters who we worked with was Bill Simmonds, who had done many years on the Western Region and was a capable and efficient railwayman. Whatever type of emergency might arise during the course of train running, Bill could always be relied upon to do the right thing and take the right action. His main concern was always the travelling public, and because of this he often incurred the disfavour of the Southern traffic controllers during the morning and evening rush-hour periods. Bill just could not see somebody running for the train and leave without them, so he would wait half a minute or so to enable them to catch it. It didn't take long to be two or three minutes late, and the message soon reached Control. If the train had made a right time start, and arrived at Waterloo a few minutes late, unless the panel box at Feltham could explain the delay, then someone would meet the train at Waterloo and ask the guard for an explanation. Bill would always tell them that the volume of passenger traffic waiting for doors to close etc. had caused the delay, and that he didn't think that two or three minutes should be considered very important in a day of twenty four hours, especially when it meant the difference between being nice to people, or leaving them panting on the platform. To his credit, he never altered, and even the controllers eventually came to understand that Bill was a competent railwayman, who would go on doing his job in the manner that he considered was correct.

During a period of severe frost and snow, Bill and I were working a train from Ascot to Guildford, and with severe icing of the conductor rail we were making slow progress. In this type of weather all train crews had come to accept that they would have a struggle getting from Bagshot to Camberley; many had come to grief somewhere on the bank from Bagshot, and had to wait for assistance from another following train. We had taken about fifty minutes to reach Camberley, — normally a six minute run — and on arrival at Guildford we chatted about the delay and discussed several ideas of our own to overcome the problem of icing of the conductor rail. A low voltage lead from the conductor rail to the running rail and back to the conductor rail might warm it sufficiently to prevent a freeze up, or running the train pick-up shoes in the side of the conductor rail instead of on the exposed surface might do the trick; but any ideas of this nature would be rejected because of cost. During the course of our chat, I happened to say that the people who built Bagshot Station should have put it about 300 yards nearer to Ascot, then we would have a downhill run of about 300 yards before meeting the stiff climb up the bank. As it was, as soon as we attempted to move from the station, we were in the start of the gradient.

The next morning the weather was still severe, and coming up to the cab at Ascot, Bill, using his Western Region parlance, said to me 'Jim, when we get to Bagshot and are ready to leave, why don't you ask the 'Bobby' if we can set back about 300 yards and start from there'. I agreed it was a good idea, if the signalman would give us permission. I doubted that he would, but would try anyway. When we were ready at Bagshot I went to the telephone on the signal close by and asked the signalman, explaining that we thought it would make all the difference in the time it took to reach Camberley. To my surprise he said 'Certainly driver, you have my permission to set back, it's no use to us to have a train in a section for fifty minutes or more wondering what has happened'. We then set back right through the roadway bridges, where the rail was protected, and then started from there. We were doing over 30m.p.h. through Bagshot Station, and although we struggled a bit near the tunnel at the top of the bank we were in Camberley in twelve minutes; it was a successful manoeuvre.

As we came through Bagshot Station a couple of late runners came charging over the bridge thinking they had just made it. We heard later that they had complained that the train didn't stop, but the staff on the 'up' side probably explained why. From that time, if there was icing of the conductor rail and it was causing trouble in the area, I always asked the signalman at Feltham if I could set back at Bagshot, as it was always a helpful and time-saving operation.

Sometime around 1966 or 1967 I was working a train over the Ascot to Aldershot line, during a very warm sunny spell in the summer. I stopped at Frimley Station, which was where the 'up' and 'down' trains usually passed each other, and a young mother came through the booking office on to the platform and had intended to walk over the footbridge to catch the 'up' train. She had a baby in her arms, and a little boy of about three years of age alongside her. My driving cab was right by the steps of the footbridge and the young woman, noticing that her train was approaching the 'up' platform, started to run with the little boy holding on to her skirt. At the bottom of the footbridge the youngster stumbled and almost fell and down came his mother's skirt, leaving her standing there in one item of underwear. I jumped out of the cab and said 'I'll take the baby', and with her skirt re-hoisted, together we hurried over to the other train, which she managed to catch. No other conversation took place as there was really no time, but I am sure that if that lady is ever asked about her most embarrassing moment, she will recall the incident at Frimley Station.

The one major incident in 1965, which will always stay in my mind, was the funeral of Sir Winston Churchill. The special train to Hanborough in Oxfordshire was due to leave Waterloo between 12.30 and 1p.m., and was to run via Reading New Junction on to the Western Region. By coincidence my brother Jack's normal roster on that day was the 12.28p.m. Waterloo to Reading service, and my own rostered duty was to work the 12.58p.m. train over the same road, so one of us would be running in front of the funeral train and the other would be following it. Because of delays in the scheduled timing of the funeral cortege, I was signalled to leave Waterloo at the right time, and although the special train must have been almost ready to leave I was running on the 'down' Windsor through line, just ahead of the funeral train. I remember the day particularly because it was so bitterly cold, but in spite of this the streets around Waterloo Station and the large concourse there were crowded with elderly and middle-aged people, who had come through the war with the great man and obviously intended to pay their last respects. Many people that I saw would have been much better off by their firesides, as the biting wind and very low temperatures must have been dangerous to them, but in spite of the weather they turned out in their thousands. Approaching the first station, Vauxhall, although I was running to Feltham first stop, I had to slow right down in speed because not only were the platforms crowded from end to end but the sloping ramps at the ends of the platforms were also crowded. It was the same at Queenstown Road, Clapham Junction, Wandsworth Town, Putney and Barnes. Every bridge and vantage point was also crowded, and in the area of Barnes Station the railway banks were crowded to a distance of two or three hundred yards outside the station. It was a most impressive experience. At Barnes I was diverted via the Brentford and Hounslow loop line, so that the special train had the pathway via Richmond and Twickenham, but I was standing at Hounslow Junction in time to see the passing of the funeral train as it ran between Whitton Junction and Feltham Junction, on its way to Reading.

CHAPTER NINE

Goodbye to Southern Steam —
Derailment at Clapham —
Class 508 Stock

The day of 10th July 1967 brought about a complete change on
the South-Western Division of the Southern Region as the last of
the Southern main lines, from Waterloo to Weymouth via Woking,
Basingstoke, Southampton and Bournemouth, saw the end of the
years of steam locomotion. New types of electric stock covered
the service to Bournemouth, where a Class 33 diesel locomotive
was attached to a portion of the train to be worked forward to
Weymouth. The line to Salisbury also surrendered its steam engines, and the new service was covered by diesel traction.

The transition, in the middle of the peak summer service, was a
meritable achievement. The heavy training programme involved in
the previous months meant that the steam men at Nine Elms, Guildford, Basingstoke, Eastleigh, Bournemouth and Weymouth had to
take on the new traction, and also satisfy the training school inspectors that they were competent to run the new trains. The new
rosters involved complete changes for all depots on the division,
and depots like Reading, Farnham and Ascot (electric) were to
undergo a loss of traditional working rosters. In the cases of
Farnham and Ascot, four men at each depot were made redundant
because work was taken from their depots to make up the new
rosters which had to accommodate all the steam men.

Reading's work up to that time was mostly over the Reading to
Waterloo line, generally Reading to Waterloo and back twice.
Most other duties included Reading to Waterloo, Alton to Waterloo,
Waterloo to Reading or Ascot to Guildford and Guildford to
Waterloo. With the new rosters we had to learn Staines to Windsor,
Staines to Weybridge and the line known as 'around the world'
which was the circular route via Twickenham, Kingston, New
Malden and back to Waterloo. Although we did not like it at the
time, events have shown that the additional route knowledge has
been of assistance to Reading men over the intervening years. It
was strange to see some of the new trains running with an engine on

the rear; some of the Class 33 locomotives and Class 73 electro-diesel locomotives could be attached to the new main line stock, and controlled from the normal electric train driving cabs. In fact, they are still working this push-pull type of running on the main line from Waterloo to Weymouth. Altogether between 850 and 900 steam men, including those stationed at Feltham and Fratton, were trained on new forms of traction, and the movement of men to new depots meant a heavy commitment to route learning at the same time.

One amusing story I heard around that time, was about two Western Region drivers from Old Oak Common, who were learning the road across to Clapham Junction and into Clapham Yard. They were walking in the yard at Clapham, with trains passing on the 'up' and 'down' Windsor side through and local lines, and on the other side the 'up' and 'down' main line through and local lines. Beyond that, trains to and from Victoria were also running up and down. The two drivers had agreed that they were in a dangerous area, and that they would have to watch themselves as there seemed to be trains everywhere. One of the new trains came past them on the 'up' main through line, with a Class 33 diesel engine on the back of the train. One of the drivers said to the other 'I'm not particular about working over here mate, look at that bloke, he must be doing forty miles an hour and he's only shunting'. I feel the tale must be true, as it was the second driver who related it to the Clapham shunt driver in the messroom shortly afterwards.

I'm not sure if it's my imagination or if it is a fact that December has, over a period of many years, been a bad month for railway accidents. It is not my intention to catalogue them here but if it is a correct assumption, there seems to be no logical reason for it. Inclement weather can often be the explanation in some cases but generally, in this country, the months of January and February produce the most hazardous weather conditions, yet December has seemed to be the dangerous month.

On 19th December 1975 there was a derailment on the 'down' Windsor through line, between Clapham Junction and Wandsworth Town stations. The train concerned was a Waterloo to Waterloo, known to all concerned with working them as 'loops', meaning that the services ran via Barnes, Richmond, Twickenham, Hounslow, Brentford, Chiswick, Barnes and then back to Waterloo. The alternate service left Waterloo a few minutes later, and ran the opposite way round the loop line from Barnes. The driver of the derailed train was a Reading driver, Derek Allen, with whom I had worked many miles on steam engines when he was a fireman, and we were

On 19th December 1975, between Clapham and Wandsworth Tunnel, while driving unit No. 7420, I pass the derailed No. 5675 with a 5in. clearance between the trains.

both in the steam depot. The photograph on the left was taken by Ray Ruffell, who was the guard of the train, and by coincidence Ray Ruffell had also been a fireman at Reading, and he had also worked with me a good many times on the footplate. Unfortunately, Ray's locomotive and motive power enthusiasm was curtailed because of serious back trouble, but he was determined to stay with train workings and became a very efficient guard. The train on the left is travelling towards Clapham Junction Station, located on the 'up' Windsor local line, while the next line over is the 'up' Windsor through line; it can be seen that the derailed train is seriously fouling this line. The derailed train is standing on the 'down' Windsor through line, with the train I was driving on the far right, running on the 'down' Windsor local line with a Reading service train. The accident occurred on a Saturday morning, at about 9.15a.m. Talking to Driver Derek Allen later, he explained that he felt two snatches and decided to stop, although he couldn't see what was happening behind him. It is possible that this coincided with the severe fracturing at the derailment between the first and second coach, which would have caused a rupturing of the continuous brake pipe and an immediate brake application.

As soon as the driver realised the seriousness of the situation he took the red flag and detonators and ran forward, to stop any train that might be travelling on the 'up' Windsor through line. Another alert railwayman, who had been a passenger on the derailed train, was running behind the driver because he also appreciated the danger to any 'up' train. On arrival at the first signal protecting the 'up' line, the driver handed detonators and flags to the other responsible man, requesting him to continue exhibiting the red flag and to proceed to Wandsworth Town Station and place detonators on the 'up' through line. The driver used the signal telephone and instructed the signalman to place all 'up' through line signals at 'danger', at the same time informing him of what had occurred. I was standing at Clapham Junction Station with the 'down' Reading service, and after considerable deliberation it was decided by the inspectors in charge that there was sufficient room for a 'down' train to pass the derailed train, under extreme caution and at walking speed. As I approached to just a few yards from the nearest point of contact between the two trains, I could see that any passenger who attempted to look out would be in extreme danger. Because of this I stopped, and asked the guard to warn all passengers not to look out under any circumstances until the train had passed the derailed train. Although we crawled by safely, Derek Allen told me that the running board on my train did actually come into contact with the other train at one point. It was afterwards decided that it was too close for comfort to attempt to continue running 'down' traffic in this way, but fortunately there was a sensible alternative. The siding next to the 'down' local line was electrified, and after clearing it of berthed coaches it was possible to run trains from Clapham Junction Station through this siding, returning to the 'down' line via a ground signal nearer to Wandsworth Town Station.

To be sure about the cause of the derailment is difficult; although a full inquiry is always held, the participants in the inquiry are seldom told of the findings. It was known that the Permanent Way Department had major engineering works in that area over the weekend, and that certain men were trying to do a few jobs in daylight which might have been difficult in darkness. One of these jobs was the slackening of certain bolts on point locking bars and stretcher bars — perhaps the wrong bolts had been slackened, or the right bolts had been slackened to a greater extent than was intended. It seems that the weight of the train passing over the points caused a slight opening of the tongue of the points, and that at one stage there was sufficient opening, with the slackened bolts, to allow a wheel to get to the wrong side of the tongue of the points. Once this occurred, the derailment was inevitable.

In 1980 we were introduced to the new 508 stock, although some of the London depots may have started training on them towards the end of 1979. We were informed that these trains had been working as three car units on the Merseyrail system in the Liverpool and Birkenhead area, and that an additional coach was added before they came to the Southern Region. Each four car unit will couple to any other unit of the same stock, but cannot be coupled to any other stock or engines, except in exceptional circumstances; for example, in the event of a complete failure.

There were many new features in the 508 stock; with the proper observation of certain regulations, the gentle coming together of two units would ensure an attachment of all functions between units, so that two four car trains became one eight car train. This sytem of 'tightlock' automatic coupling, whereby all necessary electrical contacts were made when the two units came together, was important in an area where considerable detaching and attaching was necessary because of the peak and off-peak services.

Other new features were sliding compartment doors, which are under the control of the guard of the train, a wheel-slip prevention device and the dynamic or Rheostatic braking system. The mechanics of the dynamic braking were an interesting feature whereby the traction motors are isolated from the conductor rail, and connected so that they act as generators. The current generated by this method is then passed through certain resistances, with the retarding torque being used for braking.

The drivers at Waterloo, Wimbledon Park and Strawberry Hill were the men who worked most regularly on the 508 stock, and during the autumn and early winter leaf fall, in certain areas where leaves on the running rail were a traditional nuisance, serious braking difficulties were being experienced when working the new trains. The attention of management was drawn to the problem by representatives of the drivers at local level, and certain meetings were arranged with engineers and other experts with knowledge of the trains, to decide exactly what the problem was and to discover the currect method to overcome it.

With the traditional electric train braking systems, the leaf fall period had always caused problems which were a very costly business. Braking in an area where leaves settled on the surface of the running rail would invariably cause certain wheels in the train to 'pick-up' or lock, causing serious damage to the tyre or running circumference of each locked wheel, and also damaging the surface of the running rail. The result of this locking of wheels, is 'flats', and trains with serious 'flats' have to be withdrawn from service for attention. The cost of this each autumn and winter must amount to thousands of pounds.

The 508 stock is fitted with a device to overcome wheelspin or slipping when starting, and wheelslide or locking of wheels when braking. The system performs according to the tendency of the wheels to spin or slide; if the wheels tend to spin, the application of power to the motors is cut off, but if the wheels lock during braking, the air is automatically exhausted from the brake cylinders on the axle or axles that are locked. The problem for drivers during the inclement weather was the wheel slide device, as braking on a fairly long stretch caused the wheel slide control to operate continuously, so that the proper and expected retardation of the train speed did not always occur. Many drivers felt that the problem was partly created by the fact that there were only three steps or positions for service braking applications on the driver's brake controller. It was the opinion of these men that the first position did not apply enough retardation, and that the second position was too fierce in bad rail conditions, thus causing a tendency to locked wheels, the automatic operation of the wheel slide device, and the exhausting of air from the brake cylinders.

With the traditional electro-pneumatic brake that drivers were used to, a careful and thinking driver could apply the brakes in small stages and, in many cases, avoid the locking of wheels in spite of rail conditions. To the credit of management and the engineers concerned, many exhaustive tests were made with ordinary drivers operating the brakes to their own style or choosing, and certain alterations were made to the wheel slide device which helped to overcome the problem. Eventually it was discovered what appeared to be the major cause of the trouble that drivers were experiencing when braking on a leaf-fall rail surface.

The traditional means of brake operation on British trains is by the pressure of brake blocks on the tyre, or the running circumference of each wheel fitted with brake blocks; this ensured that the running surfaces of the wheels were kept clean. The 508 stock is fitted with pad and disc brakes, and the pressure of the pads on the discs is applied at the inner sides of the wheels. This means that the running surface of the wheels was being altered, to a considerable extent, by the adhesion of resin and other chemicals from crushed leaves, and the fact that spinning wheels of many trains over falling leaves was forming a sort of carbon which tended, at times, to attach to train wheels. With brake blocks fitted, it didn't stay there long, but on 508 stock it was compressing and hardening on to wheel surfaces, and was greatly reducing the effect of retardation between wheels and rail, because a false surface on each wheel was interfering with it.

The 508 stock was no trouble during general rail conditions; in fact it was, in my opinion, very nice to work on. Although there were many features that were entirely new to all of us, various problems with the sliding doors seemed to be the most prevalent of the teething troubles. I believe the braking problems have now been sorted out to the satisfaction of all concerned, and as the trains are designed to be converted to one-man operation, this type of stock will probably serve the Southern Region commuter services for many years.

CHAPTER TEN

Dreams

Looking back to the days when almost every station had its own sidings, and every private coal merchant and colliery owned their own coal wagons, it was like reading a book to see the passing of a long freight train. Each coal wagon bearing the name of the colliery on the side, and each privately-owned wagon with the name and home station of the owner, could be as educational as a geography lesson.

There have certainly been many changes in the railway system over the past 45 years, and regardless of the fact that railways were invented in this country, it seems to me that several of our neighbouring European countries have made a far better job of developing their railway systems over the years than we have. This is also reflected in the fact that workers on Continental railways still retain a pride in their jobs — something that has been sadly absent with railwaymen in this country for years. It would be difficult to pinpoint the reasons for this, but it seems to be that no Government since 1946 has had the courage or foresight to determine a definite programme for complete integration of road and rail traffic and then to see it through.

Many factors must come into any argument on the subject, but perhaps the most important would be the interference with the environment, generally by the increase, over the past ten years, of the 'juggernaut' lorries on British roads. Not only are they moving loads that could be better handled by railways, but their increasing numbers are definitely becoming a hazard by the amount of pollution from exhaust fumes and the number of motorway accidents in which they are involved. The increase in the numbers of people that are killed and seriously injured in motor coach accidents on British roads during 1982 and 1983 seems to be acceptable, and there is no doubt that the main reason for the fact that more people are travelling by this means is that it is cheaper than by rail. I feel there is no justification for claiming that we are a caring nation if the death and injury on British roads is allowed to continue when the railways, which are publicly-owned, could be used to alleviate the problem to a great extent. I believe that the complete electrification of the whole of British Rail should be a top priority, and that rail travel should be made more accessible to the general public. The loss of life and limb would be reduced and the environment would be improved, — surely something we could all be pleased about.

Although about fourteen months have passed since I was last in charge of a train, there are occasions when I feel that I'd like to sit in the seat again, just to prove that I can still do it, but with the passing of time the feeling is with me less often. The one thing that I think will stay with me is the realisation that I do miss the men I worked with, along with the banter and backchat that was all part of the job. I have no doubt that all men who retire from a job after many years have to adjust to a new situation, but I would consider that railwaymen who have worked together for long periods of time tend to develop an *esprit de corps* that would not be common to all types of job. In one respect I am fortunate in having two sons as train drivers, as I am able to keep in touch with what is going on both locally and nationally. I am also able to chat with my old driver friends Bill Lund, Dick Lester, Ralph Powell and Tom Flight, all in their eighties, but with sharp memories of certain steam experiences in which we were involved.

In spite of the years that have passed, steam engines still hold my affection, and I never miss the chance to see one in working order. I have no idea of the vagaries of the subconscious mind, but often in that dreamy state which just precedes the onset of sleep, I am on the footplate of a steam engine, sometimes I'm the driver, and sometimes the fireman. In the more frightening dreams, that seem to come with deep sleep and often recur, I find myself charging at speed with brake failure towards the back of another train, always with a steam engine and always with me as the driver. So far I have managed to wake up without getting hurt, but what puzzles me is that it's always a steam engine — although I haven't worked on one for nineteen years.